The Simplified Book About WordPress Design And Development For Pros and Beginners:

Unlock the Secrets to Building and Customizing Professional Websites with Ease

Denita Reeds

Table of Contents

Introduction

WordPress has become one of the most popular and versatile platforms for website design and development, offering a user-friendly approach to building a powerful online presence. For many, it is the go-to tool when it comes to creating websites that are both functional and aesthetically pleasing. Whether you are launching a personal blog, setting up an online store, or developing a full-fledged business website, WordPress offers an expansive range of features, themes, and plugins that make the process relatively straightforward. But what really makes WordPress stand out is its ability to cater to a vast range of users, from complete beginners to experienced professionals. It offers both simplicity and complexity, depending on how deep you want to dive.

For beginners, WordPress presents an intuitive interface that allows for easy customization, whether it's adjusting theme settings or uploading content. On the other hand, for seasoned developers and designers, it provides a robust backend that allows for advanced customization and integration. The platform's versatility is its greatest strength; it can be as simple or as intricate as you want it to be. The depth of knowledge required to master WordPress truly may vary, but regardless of your level, WordPress offers countless opportunities for building highly functional and visually appealing websites.

While some might start their WordPress journey with minimal understanding, over time, they begin to realize that having a solid grasp of both basic and advanced concepts is essential for unlocking the full potential of the platform. Understanding how themes, plugins, and widgets work together is crucial, but so is the ability to tweak and customize code when necessary. The more you understand WordPress's mechanics, the more control you have over your website, ensuring it meets your exact needs, whether for personal or professional use.

The goal of this book is to cater to both beginners and seasoned WordPress professionals. If you're starting, you'll find step-by-step guidance on how to get your website off the ground. As you progress, you'll be introduced to more advanced topics that allow you to elevate your website's functionality and design to a higher level. At its core, this book is designed to be accessible and useful to anyone, regardless of their prior knowledge of web design or development. For beginners, the content breaks down WordPress's complexities in a simple, understandable way, while for professionals, it provides the tools and insights necessary to leverage WordPress's full potential.

The book's structure is crafted to make learning WordPress engaging and manageable. Each chapter builds on the last, starting with the foundational elements that you need to know before diving into customization and optimization. The progression of the content follows a natural learning curve, ensuring that you never feel overwhelmed but are constantly challenged to improve. The approach is hands-on, with practical examples and tips designed to give you the confidence to create websites that not only look good but also function seamlessly.

Throughout the book, you'll encounter detailed explanations of WordPress's most important features, from themes and plugins to advanced customization options using HTML, CSS, and PHP. The explanations are written with clarity, so you won't be left scratching your head, even when tackling more advanced subjects. At the same time, each chapter offers expert insights that are sure to help even the most experienced developers refine their skills. The practical examples you'll find in this book are aimed at helping you understand how to apply your knowledge in real-world situations, ensuring you can create websites that meet professional standards.

By the time you finish reading, you will have gained not only the foundational knowledge to set up your website but also the advanced skills needed to take full control of your site's design and functionality. You will learn how to build a site from scratch, customize its appearance, optimize it for search engines, and even set up an online store. This book empowers you to take your WordPress skills to new heights, giving you the tools to build websites that serve your personal or business goals.

Expect to learn how to choose the right theme for your website, install and configure essential plugins, create and manage content, and ensure your site's performance is top-notch. You will also gain a deep understanding of WordPress's more advanced features, such as customization using custom post types, integrating third-party services, and troubleshooting common issues. If you ever find yourself stuck, this book provides clear solutions that guide you back on track, ensuring that you can build with confidence.

In short, this book is designed not only as a guide but as a resource you can return to time and time again. It is meant to be more than just a one-time read—it is a tool that will support you throughout your WordPress journey, regardless of your experience level. Whether you are just beginning to explore the world of WordPress or you are looking for ways to enhance your existing skills further, this book will help you achieve your goals. By the end, you will have the knowledge and confidence to create stunning, functional, and successful WordPress websites, no matter your skill level.

Chapter 1: Understanding WordPress – A Comprehensive Introduction

WordPress is a powerful and flexible content management system (CMS) that allows users to create and manage websites with ease. Initially launched in 2003, it has grown from a simple blogging tool to one of the most popular platforms for building websites of all kinds, ranging from personal blogs to large-scale business websites and e-commerce stores. Today, WordPress powers more than 40% of all websites on the internet, a testament to its usability, flexibility, and constant evolution. This chapter will introduce you to WordPress, explain its history and evolution, highlight the difference between WordPress.com and WordPress.org, explore the key features and advantages of using WordPress for website design, delve into the understanding of themes, plugins, and widgets, and discuss the open-source nature of WordPress and the incredible community that supports it.

What is WordPress? A Brief History and Evolution

At its core, WordPress is an open-source CMS designed for creating websites. Open-source means that WordPress's source code is freely available for anyone to use, modify, and distribute, encouraging innovation and collaboration. Originally launched as a blogging platform by Matt Mullenweg and Mike Little in 2003, WordPress allowed users to create and manage blogs in a user-friendly way. Over time, however, WordPress evolved far beyond its humble beginnings. It soon became a fully-fledged CMS, allowing users to design and manage complex websites with little to no coding experience.

The evolution of WordPress can be traced through its numerous updates and releases, each introducing new features that made it easier to customize websites. One key milestone in its development was the release of the WordPress plugin system in 2004, which allowed developers to extend WordPress's functionality. This opened up endless possibilities for customization, and soon, third-party developers began creating themes, plugins, and widgets that enhanced the user experience.

Today, WordPress is one of the most widely used CMS platforms in the world, not just for blogging but for everything from e-commerce sites and portfolios to corporate websites and news outlets. Its versatility and ease of use have made it the preferred choice for millions of users, from beginners to professional developers. The constant development of features and functionality, as well as an extensive community of developers and users, ensures that WordPress will remain at the forefront of website creation for years to come.

Difference Between WordPress.com and WordPress.org

One of the most common sources of confusion among WordPress users, especially beginners, is the difference between WordPress.com and WordPress.org. While both platforms share the WordPress name, they are quite different in terms of how they operate and what they offer.

WordPress.com is a hosted platform that takes care of everything for you. It's a subscription-based service where users can create a website without having to worry about installation, hosting, or maintenance. When you sign up for WordPress.com, you get access to a WordPress-powered website, but with some limitations. For example, WordPress.com provides a set of pre-designed themes and plugins, but you cannot upload custom themes or plugins unless you opt for a higher-tier plan. Additionally, the free version of WordPress.com places ads on your site, and you cannot monetize it until you upgrade to a premium plan.

On the other hand, WordPress.org is the self-hosted version of WordPress. This means that users must download the WordPress software and install it on their web server or hosting provider. With WordPress.org, you have complete control over your website, including the ability to install custom themes and plugins, edit code, and access advanced features that are not available on WordPress.com. However, it also means that you are responsible for maintaining your website, managing updates, and ensuring that your hosting environment is secure. While WordPress.org requires more technical knowledge, it offers unparalleled flexibility and is the preferred option for those who want to have full control over their website.

In summary, WordPress.com is ideal for users who want an easy-to-use platform with minimal setup and maintenance, while WordPress.org is better suited for users who want more control and flexibility over their website. Most advanced users and businesses opt for WordPress.org due to its vast customization options, ability to monetize websites, and full control over their online presence.

Key Features and Advantages of WordPress for Website Design

WordPress offers a wide range of features and advantages that make it an ideal choice for website design, regardless of the user's experience level. Some of the key features that make WordPress stand out include:

1. **Ease of Use**: One of the main reasons WordPress is so popular is that it is incredibly user-friendly. Even users with little to no technical knowledge can create and manage a website. The WordPress dashboard is intuitive and easy to navigate, allowing users to manage

their website's content, design, and settings from a central location.

2. **Customizable Themes**: WordPress offers a vast library of themes, both free and premium, which can be used to change the look and feel of your website. Themes are pre-designed templates that dictate the layout, structure, and visual elements of your website. Whether you want a minimalistic design or a more intricate layout, there are themes available for virtually every type of website.

3. **Plugins for Functionality**: WordPress plugins are extensions that add functionality to your website. From SEO tools and social media integration to contact forms and security features, plugins allow you to customize and enhance your website's performance. With thousands of plugins available, you can add almost any feature you need, without having to write a single line of code.

4. **Responsive Design**: WordPress themes are designed to be mobile-friendly and responsive, meaning they will adjust automatically to look

great on any device. This is important because more and more people access websites via smartphones and tablets. With WordPress, you don't need to worry about ensuring your website is mobile-compatible—most themes handle this automatically.

5. **SEO-Friendly**: WordPress is built with search engine optimization (SEO) in mind. It provides various tools and features that help improve your website's ranking on search engines like Google. From customizable permalinks and meta descriptions to SEO plugins like Yoast, WordPress makes it easier to optimize your content and drive organic traffic to your site.

6. **Content Management**: WordPress's simple yet powerful editor makes content management easy. Whether you're writing blog posts, creating product pages, or adding multimedia, the WordPress content editor is intuitive and easy to use. It also allows you to schedule posts, create drafts, and organize content with categories and tags.

7. **Security**: WordPress takes security seriously and provides a range of tools and practices to ensure that your website stays safe. Regular updates to the WordPress core, themes, and plugins help patch any security vulnerabilities. Additionally, numerous security plugins are available to add extra layers of protection, such as firewalls, malware scanners, and login attempt limits.

8. **Community Support**: WordPress has a vast community of users, developers, and designers who contribute to its growth and support. If you encounter an issue or need help, you can find answers in the official WordPress forums, online tutorials, blogs, and even social media groups. The active community ensures that WordPress stays updated and provides ongoing support for users at all levels.

Understanding Themes, Plugins, and Widgets

Themes, plugins, and widgets are the building blocks of WordPress websites. Understanding how these components work is essential to creating a fully functional and customized site.

- **Themes**: As mentioned earlier, themes define the visual appearance of your website. WordPress themes control everything from the layout and color scheme to fonts and overall design. There are thousands of free and premium themes available, catering to a variety of needs. When selecting a theme, it's important to consider factors like responsiveness, customization options, and compatibility with plugins. A good theme can drastically improve the aesthetics and functionality of your website.

- **Plugins**: Plugins are extensions that add specific features or functionality to your website. Whether you need to add a contact form, integrate with social media, optimize for SEO, or improve website speed, there is likely a plugin for the task. WordPress plugins are easy to install and configure, making them a great tool for enhancing your website's capabilities. However, it's important not to overload your site with too many plugins, as they can slow down performance.

- **Widgets**: Widgets are small blocks of content or functionality that can be added to your website's sidebar, footer, or other widget-ready areas. Widgets allow you to display various elements, such as recent posts, calendars, social media feeds, or custom HTML. These elements can be easily managed from the WordPress dashboard without needing to modify any code.

The Open-Source Nature of WordPress and Its Community Support

One key aspect that sets WordPress apart from other website-building platforms is its open-source nature. WordPress is free to use, and anyone can contribute to its development. This open-source model allows developers from all around the world to improve the platform, create plugins, and develop themes that benefit the entire WordPress community.

The WordPress community is vast and diverse, consisting of users, developers, designers, and contributors who share knowledge and support one another. This community-driven approach has led to the continuous evolution of WordPress, with frequent updates, security patches, and new features being added. Additionally, there are countless online resources, tutorials, forums, and support groups where users can find help and share their experiences. Whether you're a beginner or an experienced developer, the WordPress community is there to guide you every step of the way.

WordPress's open-source nature, coupled with its strong community support, is one of the major reasons for its success. It allows users to have full control over their websites while benefiting from the collective knowledge and resources of the global WordPress community.

This chapter introduces you to the essentials of WordPress, providing a solid foundation for further learning. By understanding the platform's history, differences between WordPress.com and WordPress.org, and the key features that make it so powerful, you will be better prepared to dive into the details of website design and development. The next chapters will build on this knowledge, offering you the tools and insights needed to create your own WordPress website with confidence.

Chapter 2: Getting Started with WordPress – Setting Up Your First Website

Starting your first website on WordPress can be both exciting and overwhelming. Fortunately, WordPress is designed to be user-friendly and can help you create a stunning website with minimal effort. In this chapter, we'll guide you through the essential steps of setting up your first WordPress site, from choosing and registering your domain name to navigating the WordPress dashboard and adjusting key settings. By the end of this chapter, you'll know how to get your WordPress site up and running smoothly.

How to Choose and Register a Domain Name

Choosing the right domain name is one of the most important steps in creating your website. Your domain name is your online address—essentially, it's how people will find you on the internet. Therefore, it's crucial to choose a name that represents your brand or business, is easy to remember, and is relevant to the content you plan to share.

1. **Choosing a Domain Name:** Start by brainstorming a list of potential names that represent your brand, blog, or business. Your domain name should be simple, catchy, and easy to spell. Ideally, it should reflect your content or niche. For example, if you're starting a photography business, your domain name might include terms like "photo," "images," or "pictures." If you're creating a personal blog, consider using your name or a unique phrase that reflects your interests.

A good domain name is:

- o Short and simple: Shorter names are easier to remember and type.

- o Relevant: Your domain should give users an idea of what your website is about.

- o Unique: Avoid names that are too similar to existing websites, as this can confuse.

- o Avoid hyphens and numbers: They can be hard to remember and often confuse users.

2. **Checking Domain Name Availability:** Once you've come up with a potential domain name, check its availability. Numerous online tools can help you search for available domain names. You can also use domain name generators to get more suggestions based on your initial idea. If the name you want has already been taken, you may need to get creative by adding keywords, using a different domain extension (like .net or .co), or modifying the name slightly.

3. **Registering Your Domain Name:** After you've selected a domain name that's available, it's time to register it. To do this, you'll need to go through a domain registrar, which is a company that manages the reservation of domain names. Some popular domain registrars include GoDaddy, Namecheap, and Bluehost. Domain registration usually costs between $10 and $20 per year, depending on the domain extension (.com, .org, etc.).

Most domain registrars also offer the option to purchase additional services, such as domain privacy protection, which helps keep your personal information private and prevents unwanted solicitations. Once you've purchased your domain, you'll receive login credentials that allow you to manage your domain settings.

Selecting a Hosting Provider and Setting Up Your WordPress Site

Choosing a reliable hosting provider is crucial to ensuring that your website runs smoothly and performs well. A hosting provider stores all your website's files and makes them accessible to users over the internet. Without a good hosting service, your website could be slow, experience downtime, or even become inaccessible.

1. **What is Web Hosting?** Web hosting is a service that allows you to publish your website on the internet. When you buy web hosting, you essentially rent space on a server where your website's files are stored. These servers are powerful machines that handle all the data requests from visitors who want to view your website. Hosting providers also offer features such as security, support, and scalability.

2. **Types of Hosting:** There are several types of hosting to choose from, and the right one for you depends on your needs, budget, and technical expertise. The most common types of hosting include:

  o **Shared Hosting**: This is the most affordable option. With shared hosting, your website shares a server with other websites. While it's a good choice for beginners and small websites, the performance can be affected if the server is crowded.

  o **VPS Hosting**: Virtual Private Server (VPS) hosting is a step up from shared hosting. It gives you more control over your server environment, allowing you to customize the settings for better performance. VPS hosting is suitable for growing websites that require more resources.

  o **Dedicated Hosting**: With dedicated hosting, you get an entire server to yourself. This option is ideal for large websites with heavy traffic or complex requirements. However, it's also the most expensive option.

- o **Managed WordPress Hosting**: Managed hosting is a premium service where the hosting provider takes care of everything related to your WordPress site, including performance optimization, security, updates, and backups. Managed hosting is a great choice for users who want to focus on their content and leave the technical aspects to professionals.

3. **Selecting a Hosting Provider:** When choosing a hosting provider, it's important to consider factors such as uptime reliability, customer support, ease of use, and scalability. Some popular hosting providers for WordPress include Bluehost, SiteGround, and HostGator. Many of these providers offer one-click WordPress installation, which makes it easy to get started with minimal effort.

- o **WordPress.org** **officially recommends Bluehost** and offers affordable plans with great support.

- o **SiteGround** is known for its excellent performance and customer service.

- o **HostGator** offers flexible pricing and a range of plans to suit different needs.

Once you've selected a hosting provider, you'll need to sign up for a hosting plan and follow the instructions to link your domain name to the hosting account. This typically involves changing your domain's nameservers to point to your hosting provider's server.

4. **Setting Up WordPress:** After purchasing your hosting plan and registering your domain name, you'll need to install WordPress. There are two primary ways to install WordPress: manual installation and one-click installation.

Installing WordPress (Manual vs. One-Click Installation)

Installing WordPress is a relatively simple process, and there are two main ways to do it: manually or through one-click installation. The method you choose will depend on your hosting provider and your level of technical expertise.

1. **One-Click Installation:** Most reputable hosting providers offer a one-click installation feature for WordPress. This feature automates the installation process, allowing you to set up your WordPress site with just a few clicks. After purchasing your hosting plan, you can typically access the one-click WordPress installer from your hosting control panel (often referred to as cPanel).

With a one-click installation, you select your domain, choose your WordPress settings, and click a button to start the installation. The installer will automatically download and configure WordPress, so you won't need to worry about uploading files or configuring databases. This method is ideal for beginners who don't have technical experience.

2. **Manual Installation:** If your hosting provider doesn't offer one-click installation or you prefer a more hands-on approach, you can install WordPress manually. While this method

requires a bit more technical knowledge, it gives you more control over the installation process.

The manual installation involves downloading the WordPress software from WordPress.org, uploading the files to your server, creating a database, and running the WordPress installation script. While this process may sound complicated, detailed instructions are available on the WordPress website that can guide you through each step.

Introduction to the WordPress Dashboard: Navigating the Backend

Once WordPress is installed, you can access your website's backend through the WordPress dashboard. The dashboard is where you'll spend most of your time when managing your website. It's the central hub that allows you to control every aspect of your site, from content creation and design to settings and plugins.

1. **The WordPress Dashboard Overview:** After logging into WordPress using your admin credentials, you'll be taken to the dashboard. The dashboard is divided into several sections, including:

- o **At a Glance**: A summary of your website's current status, including the number of posts, pages, comments, and plugins installed.

- o **Activity**: Displays recent activity on your site, such as new comments or recent posts.

- o **Quick Draft**: Allows you to write a draft post or page quickly.

- o **WordPress News**: Displays the latest news and updates from the WordPress community.

2. **Navigation Menu:** On the left side of the dashboard, you'll see a vertical navigation menu. This menu provides access to all of the main sections of the WordPress backend, including:

- o **Posts**: Where you can create and manage blog posts.

- o **Pages**: Where you can create and manage static pages, such as your homepage or about page.

- Media: Where you can upload and manage images, videos, and other media files.

- Comments: Where you can manage comments left by visitors on your posts.

- Appearance: Where you can customize your website's design, including themes, widgets, and menus.

- Plugins: Where you can install and manage plugins that extend your site's functionality.

- Settings: Where you can adjust your website's settings, such as general settings, reading preferences, and more.

Understanding WordPress Settings (General, Reading, Discussion, etc.)

WordPress comes with a variety of settings that allow you to customize your website's behavior and appearance. Some of the most important settings include:

1. **General Settings**: The general settings section is where you can set your website's title, tagline, and default time zone. You can also adjust the language settings and manage user permissions.

2. **Reading Settings**: In this section, you can control how your site's content is displayed to visitors. You can choose to display a static page as your homepage or show your latest blog posts. You can also control how many posts are displayed on each page and whether search engines should index your site's content.

3. **Discussion Settings**: This section allows you to manage how comments are handled on your site. You can turn comments on or off, require approval for new comments, and set up notification preferences for comment moderation.

By following the steps outlined in this chapter, you'll be able to choose a domain name, select a hosting provider, and set up WordPress with ease. With your website up and running, you can dive deeper into customizing your site and creating engaging content. The WordPress dashboard provides all the tools you need to manage your site, and with the right settings in place, you'll be on your way to building a successful online presence.

Chapter 3: Customizing Your Website with Themes

WordPress themes are the backbone of website design, as they control the visual appearance of your site and how users interact with it. When you install WordPress, it comes with a default theme, but most website owners choose to install a new theme that reflects their brand and website's purpose. In this chapter, we will explore what WordPress themes are, how to choose the right one for your website, how to install and activate a theme, how to customize theme settings such as colors, fonts, and layouts, and how to use child themes for more advanced customization. Additionally, we'll look at how to ensure that your theme is mobile-responsive and optimized for all devices.

What Are WordPress Themes?

At its core, a WordPress theme is a collection of files that work together to create your website's design and layout. These files can include templates, stylesheets, images, and JavaScript files that dictate how your site looks, how the content is displayed, and how interactive elements function. A theme can completely change your website's visual design without affecting the content you have created.

Themes are what make WordPress so customizable. By installing a theme, you can easily change the look of your site, adjusting elements such as colors, typography, layout, and navigation structure. While WordPress's default theme offers a basic layout, a custom theme allows for much more flexibility, providing you with various options for personalization.

WordPress themes are designed to be versatile, enabling users to modify them to suit their specific needs. Depending on the theme you choose, you can either make simple tweaks through the WordPress Customizer or dive deeper into code to create highly customized designs. Themes also work with plugins, enabling you to add additional functionality to your site, such as contact forms, galleries, or e-commerce features.

Choosing the Right Theme for Your Website's Purpose

Selecting the right WordPress theme for your website is an important decision that will influence the overall look and feel of your site. The theme you choose should align with your website's goals and content while offering flexibility for customization. Here are several factors to consider when choosing the right theme for your website's purpose:

1. **Purpose of Your Website:** Start by determining the primary purpose of your website. Are you building a personal blog, a business website, an online store, or a portfolio? Each type of website has unique requirements in terms of design and functionality. For example:

   o **Personal Blog:** Choose a theme that focuses on readability, with a clean and simple layout. You may also want a theme that emphasizes your posts, allowing for easy navigation and comment management.

   o **Business Website:** A business theme should have a professional and polished appearance, with features that highlight your services, testimonials, and contact information. You might also want a theme that integrates with an appointment booking system or a lead capture form.

- o **E-commerce Website:** For online stores, look for themes designed specifically for e-commerce. These themes will include built-in support for product catalogs, shopping carts, and payment gateways. WooCommerce-compatible themes are the most common choice for WordPress e-commerce sites.

- o **Portfolio or Photography Website:** A portfolio theme should emphasize visual elements, with options for large images and galleries. It should have a minimalist layout to ensure your work takes center stage.

2. **Design and Aesthetics:** The theme's visual design should reflect your brand and the message you want to convey to your audience. If you are creating a professional website, make sure the theme offers a sleek and modern design. If your site is for personal use, you may want something more creative and unique. Look

for themes that align with your style preferences, whether that's bold and modern or minimalist and elegant.

3. **Responsiveness:** Ensure that the theme you select is mobile-responsive. More and more people are accessing websites on mobile devices, so it's essential that your website looks great and functions properly on smartphones and tablets. A responsive theme automatically adjusts its layout to fit different screen sizes, improving the user experience.

4. **Customization Options:** Consider how much flexibility the theme offers in terms of customization. Some themes come with built-in customization options, such as color pickers, font choices, and layout settings, that allow you to make changes without writing any code. If you want to have more control over your site's design, look for a theme that supports custom CSS or allows you to use a page builder plugin.

5. **SEO-Friendly:** Choose a theme that is designed with search engine optimization (SEO) in mind. SEO-friendly themes are built with

clean code, fast loading times, and optimized structure, which can help improve your site's visibility on search engines like Google.

6. **Support and Documentation:** When choosing a theme, check whether it's well-supported and comes with comprehensive documentation. Premium themes often include support from the theme developer, which can be invaluable if you encounter any issues. Good documentation can also help you understand how to set up and customize your theme.

Once you've considered these factors, you can start browsing the WordPress theme repository or third-party theme providers. WordPress offers a vast selection of free themes, while premium themes are available for purchase from marketplaces like ThemeForest, StudioPress, and Elegant Themes.

Installing and Activating a Theme

Once you've chosen the right theme for your website, it's time to install and activate it. WordPress makes it easy to install themes, whether you're using a free theme from the WordPress theme repository or a premium theme you've purchased elsewhere.

1. **Installing a Theme from the WordPress Theme Repository:**

    o Go to your WordPress dashboard and navigate to **Appearance > Themes**.

    o Click on the **Add New** button at the top of the page.

    o You can either search for a theme by name or browse themes by category, features, or popularity.

    o Once you've found the theme you want to install, hover over it and click **Install**.

    o After the theme is installed, click **Activate** to make it live on your site.

2. **Installing a Premium Theme:** If you've purchased a premium theme from a third-party provider, you'll need to upload it manually. To do this:

    o Download the theme's ZIP file from the provider's website.

- o Go to your WordPress dashboard and navigate to **Appearance** > **Themes**.

- o Click on **Add New** and then select **Upload Theme**.

- o Click **Choose File**, select the ZIP file, and then click **Install Now**.

- o Once the theme is installed, click **Activate**.

After activating your theme, it will be applied to your website, but it will likely need some customization to fit your specific needs.

Customizing Your Theme Settings: Colors, Fonts, Layouts, and More

Once your theme is installed and activated, you can begin customizing it to match your brand and style. WordPress provides a built-in tool called the **Customizer**, which allows you to modify various theme settings, including colors, fonts, layouts, and more.

1. **Accessing the Customizer:** To access the Customizer, go to your WordPress dashboard

and navigate to **Appearance** > **Customize**. This will open the theme Customizer, where you can make changes to your website's design and settings.

2. **Changing Colors:** Most themes allow you to change the color scheme of your site. You can usually modify the background color, text color, link color, and button color. Look for options in the **Colors** section of the Customizer, where you can use a color picker or enter color codes to adjust the theme's color scheme.

3. **Changing Fonts:** Many themes come with built-in font options, and you can change the typography for various elements such as headings, paragraphs, and links. In the **Typography** section of the Customizer, you'll be able to select different font families, adjust font sizes, and set font weights. For more advanced control, you can use custom CSS to apply specific fonts to certain elements.

4. **Adjusting Layouts:** Depending on the theme, you may be able to modify the layout of your pages and posts. For example, you can change

the number of columns on your homepage, adjust sidebar positions, or choose between full-width and boxed layouts. Look for layout options in the **Layout** section of the Customizer.

5. **Customizing Widgets and Menus:** In the **Widgets** section of the Customizer, you can manage the various widgets that appear on your site. Widgets are small content blocks that can be placed in areas such as sidebars, footers, and headers. Common widgets include recent posts, social media feeds, and search bars.

You can also manage your website's menus from the **Menus** section of the Customizer. Here, you can create custom menus for your site's navigation and add links to pages, posts, categories, or custom URLs.

Using Child Themes for Advanced Customization

While WordPress themes are highly customizable, there may be times when you want to make more advanced changes to your theme's code. However, editing the theme's core files directly is not recommended, as it can lead to issues when the theme is updated. Instead, you should use a **child theme**.

A child theme is a sub-theme that inherits the functionality and design of the parent theme but allows you to make modifications without affecting the original theme files. By using a child theme, you can safely update your parent theme without losing your customizations.

To create a child theme, you need to:

1. Create a new folder in the **wp-content/themes** directory.

2. Add a **style.css** file that links to the parent theme's styles.

3. Add a **functions.php** file that enqueues the parent theme's styles.

Once your child theme is set up, you can add custom CSS, modify template files, and even create custom functions. This allows you to take full control over your site's design while ensuring that your customizations remain intact after theme updates.

Tips for Making Your Theme Mobile-Responsive

In today's mobile-first world, it's essential to ensure that your WordPress theme is mobile-responsive. A mobile-responsive theme automatically adjusts its layout and design to provide an optimal viewing experience on smartphones and tablets.

Here are some tips for ensuring your theme is mobile-responsive:

1. **Choose a Responsive Theme:** Most modern WordPress themes are designed to be responsive, but it's important to double-check before installing a theme. Look for a theme that is explicitly marked as "responsive" or "mobile-friendly."

2. **Test Your Site on Multiple Devices:** After customizing your theme, test how your site looks on different screen sizes. You can use tools like Google's Mobile-Friendly Test or Chrome's Developer Tools to simulate how your site will appear on mobile devices.

3. **Optimize Images:** Large, unoptimized images can slow down your site and negatively affect

the user experience, especially on mobile devices. Use image optimization plugins or services to reduce image file sizes without sacrificing quality.

4. **Avoid Fixed Width Elements:** Fixed-width elements, such as large images or wide tables, can cause issues on smaller screens. Use relative widths (e.g., percentages) instead of fixed widths (e.g., pixels) to ensure that content adapts to different screen sizes.

By following these tips, you can ensure that your WordPress theme looks great on all devices, enhancing the user experience for visitors on mobile and tablet devices.

Customizing your WordPress theme is one of the most exciting and rewarding aspects of website creation. From choosing the right theme to adjusting colors, fonts, and layouts, there are endless opportunities to personalize your site. Whether you're making basic adjustments through the WordPress Customizer or using a child theme for advanced modifications, this chapter has provided you with the tools you need to create a beautiful and functional website. With your theme fully customized, you can focus on creating content and engaging your audience.

Chapter 4: Understanding WordPress Plugins

WordPress is a powerful content management system that comes with an impressive range of features right out of the box. However, one of the key reasons behind WordPress's popularity is its ability to extend functionality through plugins. Plugins are essential tools that allow you to enhance your website's capabilities, whether you need to add a simple contact form, optimize your website for search engines, secure your site from threats, or add complex features like e-commerce capabilities. In this chapter, we will explore what WordPress plugins are, why they are essential, how to install and activate them, and some of the must-have plugins for both beginners and experienced WordPress users. We will also cover SEO plugins, performance and caching plugins, security plugins, and how to configure plugins for optimal performance.

What Are Plugins and Why Are They Essential?

Plugins are pieces of software that extend or add specific features to your WordPress website. WordPress itself comes with basic features, but plugins allow you to customize and enhance your site's functionality by adding new tools and services. These plugins range from simple enhancements like adding a contact form to more complex features such as e-commerce systems, membership systems, or multi-language support.

WordPress plugins can be written in PHP, JavaScript, HTML, and CSS and integrate seamlessly with the core WordPress platform. Anyone can develop plugins, and the WordPress Plugin Repository, available directly within the WordPress dashboard, offers thousands of plugins, both free and premium, for download.

Why are plugins essential? The answer is simple: WordPress plugins allow users to extend and enhance the functionality of their websites without needing to write a single line of code. Whether you're building a personal blog, an online store, or a corporate website, plugins provide the flexibility to add features that are tailored to your specific needs.

For instance, if you need to add a gallery to your site, instead of coding one from scratch, you can install a gallery plugin that allows you to insert and display images or videos easily. Similarly, for SEO, you don't need to configure each page for search engines manually; plugins like Yoast SEO automatically handle optimization tasks, making it easier for you to rank higher in search results.

Plugins allow WordPress users to:

- Add custom features without the need for coding knowledge.

- Improve website functionality in a variety of ways.

- Improve the user experience with added tools and services.

- Ensure that a website is optimized, secure, and running at peak performance.

In short, plugins are essential because they provide both functionality and flexibility, enabling users to customize their website to suit their needs. Without plugins, WordPress would not be as versatile or user-friendly as it is today.

Installing and Activating Plugins

Installing and activating plugins in WordPress is a straightforward process that doesn't require much technical knowledge. WordPress provides an easy-to-use plugin management system that allows users to find, install, and activate plugins directly from the WordPress dashboard. Here's a step-by-step guide on how to install and activate plugins:

1. **Log into Your WordPress Dashboard:** To get started, you must first log into the WordPress admin area by visiting www.yoursite.com/wp-admin and entering your admin credentials.

2. **Navigate to the Plugins Section:** On the left-hand sidebar of the dashboard, click on **Plugins** > **Add New**. This will take you to the plugin installation page where you can browse available plugins or search for a specific plugin.

3. **Search for the Plugin You Want to Install:** Use the search bar on the right side to find the plugin you're looking for. You can search by the plugin name or type of feature you want (e.g., SEO, contact form, caching).

4. **Install the Plugin:** Once you find the plugin you want to install, click the **Install Now**

button next to it. WordPress will automatically download and install the plugin.

5. **Activate the Plugin:** After the plugin is installed, the button will change to **Activate**. Click this button to activate the plugin on your site. Some plugins may require additional configuration after activation, which you will be prompted to complete.

6. **Configure the Plugin:** Many plugins offer configuration options to customize their functionality. These options are usually found under the **Settings** menu in the WordPress dashboard or within the plugin's own menu item on the left sidebar.

It's important to note that some plugins may require you to create accounts or connect to external services (for example, with security plugins or e-commerce plugins), so be sure to follow the plugin's instructions after activation.

Must-Have Plugins for Beginners and Pros

There are thousands of WordPress plugins available, so it can be overwhelming to figure out which ones are essential for your website. However, some plugins are considered must-haves, whether you're a beginner or a pro. These plugins are designed to help you optimize your website's performance, security, and user experience. Below is a list of must-have plugins for both beginners and advanced users:

For Beginners:

1. **Yoast SEO (Search Engine Optimization):** Yoast SEO is one of the most popular and powerful SEO plugins available for WordPress. It helps you optimize your content for search engines by providing real-time suggestions and tips for improving your pages and posts. Yoast SEO handles the technical aspects of SEO, such as meta tags, sitemaps, and breadcrumbs, and provides a user-friendly interface to ensure that your content is optimized for search engine visibility.

2. **WPForms (Contact Forms):** WPForms is an easy-to-use contact form plugin that allows you to create and manage forms on your WordPress site. Whether you need a simple contact form, a registration form, or a survey form, WPForms

provides a drag-and-drop builder that makes it easy to design forms without any coding knowledge.

3. **Akismet Anti-Spam:** Akismet is a must-have plugin for preventing spam comments on your site. It automatically checks comments and contact form submissions for spam and filters out suspicious ones. This plugin helps you maintain a clean and professional website by eliminating unwanted spam.

4. **Elementor (Page Builder):** Elementor is a drag-and-drop page builder plugin that allows you to create beautiful, custom page layouts without writing any code. With its wide range of templates and design options, Elementor is perfect for beginners who want to create stunning pages while retaining full control over their designs.

5. **UpdraftPlus (Backup Plugin):** Regular backups are essential for any website. UpdraftPlus allows you to schedule and store backups of your WordPress site on various cloud services, such as Google Drive, Dropbox,

and Amazon S3. In case of a crash or disaster, you can restore your site with just a few clicks.

For Pros:

1. **WooCommerce (E-Commerce):** If you're building an online store, WooCommerce is the go-to plugin for WordPress. It enables you to sell physical or digital products, manage inventory, and set up payment gateways, taxes, and shipping methods. WooCommerce is incredibly customizable and works well with a variety of themes and extensions.

2. **WP Rocket (Caching Plugin):** WP Rocket is a premium caching plugin designed to improve your website's performance and speed. It reduces loading times by caching static files, minifying CSS/JS, and optimizing images. WP Rocket is easy to set up and doesn't require technical knowledge, making it a popular choice for advanced users.

3. **Wordfence Security (Security Plugin):** Wordfence Security is one of the most comprehensive security plugins for WordPress. It offers features such as malware scanning,

firewall protection, and login security. Wordfence also provides real-time security alerts, so you'll always know if your site is at risk.

4. **Advanced Custom Fields (ACF):** For more advanced customization, ACF allows you to add custom fields to your WordPress posts, pages, and other content types. This plugin is ideal for developers who want to build highly custom sites or need to create complex data structures.

5. **TablePress (Tables):** TablePress is a plugin that allows you to create and manage tables on your WordPress site without any coding. It's perfect for displaying large amounts of data in a clean and organized format. You can easily import/export tables from CSV files and customize them using the built-in editor.

SEO Plugins: Yoast SEO

Search engine optimization (SEO) is crucial for driving organic traffic to your website. One of the most popular SEO plugins for WordPress is Yoast SEO. This plugin helps you optimize your site's content by providing actionable recommendations for improving on-page SEO.

Yoast SEO features:

- **Content Analysis**: Yoast analyzes your content and provides recommendations for improving SEO. It helps you optimize meta titles, descriptions, and headings and checks keyword density.

- **XML Sitemaps**: The plugin automatically generates XML sitemaps, which help search engines crawl your website more efficiently.

- **Breadcrumbs**: Yoast allows you to add breadcrumbs to your site, which enhances navigation and helps search engines understand your site's structure.

- **Social Media Integration**: The plugin helps you configure social media metadata, making it easier to share your content on platforms like Facebook and Twitter.

To configure Yoast SEO for optimal performance, follow the on-screen wizard to set up the basic settings. Be sure to enter a focus keyword for each post/page, and follow Yoast's recommendations to improve your content's SEO score.

Performance and Caching Plugins: WP Super Cache

Website speed is crucial for both user experience and SEO. Slow-loading websites can negatively impact bounce rates and search engine rankings. Caching plugins like **WP Super Cache** can significantly improve website performance by serving static files to visitors, reducing the time it takes for pages to load.

WP Super Cache generates static HTML files from your dynamic WordPress website. When a visitor comes to your site, the plugin serves the cached version of the page, resulting in faster load times. WP Super Cache is easy to configure and offers several options for customizing caching behavior, such as enabling compression and caching for mobile users.

Security Plugins: Wordfence

Hackers and malicious bots frequently target WordPress websites. To secure your website, it's essential to use a security plugin like **Wordfence**. Wordfence provides real-time protection against security threats and scans your site for malware, vulnerabilities, and other security risks.

Key features of Wordfence include:

- **Firewall Protection**: Protects your site from malicious traffic and unauthorized access.

- **Malware Scanning**: Regularly scans your site for malware and harmful code.

- **Login Security**: Offers features like two-factor authentication and CAPTCHA to prevent brute force attacks.

How to Configure Plugins for Optimal Performance

Configuring plugins for optimal performance requires understanding your website's needs and selecting plugins that align with those requirements. After installation and activation, most plugins will have a settings page where you can adjust the configuration to suit your site. Pay attention to the following tips:

- **Avoid Overloading Plugins**: Installing too many plugins can slow down your site. Only use plugins that are essential to your website's functionality.

- **Minimize Plugin Conflicts**: Some plugins may not work well together. Test plugins individually to ensure they don't affect your site's performance or layout.

- **Update Plugins Regularly**: Plugin developers frequently release updates to fix bugs, add new features, and improve security. Make sure your plugins are always up to date.

Managing and Updating Plugins to Maintain Website Functionality

Managing and updating your plugins is essential to ensure your website remains functional, secure, and optimized. You can manage all of your installed plugins by navigating to **Plugins** > **Installed Plugins** from your WordPress dashboard. Here, you can activate, deactivate, and delete plugins as needed.

To update plugins:

1. Navigate to **Dashboard** > **Updates**.

2. You'll see a list of plugins that need updating.

3. Click **Update Now** to install the latest versions of the plugins.

Check for plugin updates regularly and test your site after updating to ensure everything functions correctly. If you encounter issues, consider disabling plugins one at a time to identify the source of the problem.

Plugins are an essential part of WordPress website development. Whether you're a beginner or an experienced user, plugins offer the flexibility and functionality you need to customize and optimize your site. By understanding how plugins work and how to manage them effectively, you can ensure that your website is fast, secure, and optimized for both users and search engines.

Chapter 5: Designing Your Website – Essential WordPress Design Tools

When it comes to designing your website, WordPress offers an array of powerful tools that enable you to build a site that not only looks great but also functions seamlessly. Whether you are creating a personal blog, an e-commerce store, or a professional portfolio, the design of your website plays a crucial role in engaging your visitors, communicating your brand message, and ensuring an optimal user experience (UX). In this chapter, we will discuss the importance of user experience (UX) and user interface (UI), introduce you to popular page builders like Elementor and Gutenberg, and provide you with a step-by-step guide to creating stunning pages. We will also cover the customization of essential pages such as your homepage, about page, and contact form, and explore how to add media to your site, including images, videos, and galleries. Finally, we will look at creating and managing a blog to share content with your audience.

The Importance of User Experience (UX) and User Interface (UI)

When it comes to website design, two key concepts—user experience (UX) and user interface (UI)—play a significant role in determining the success of your website. Both UX and UI refer to how users interact with and experience your website, but they have distinct focuses.

1. **User Experience (UX):** UX refers to the overall experience that users have when interacting with your website. It is a broad concept that encompasses how easy and enjoyable it is for users to navigate your site, find information, and perform desired actions. Good UX design ensures that users have a smooth, intuitive, and satisfying experience from the moment they land on your website to the moment they leave.

Key elements of good UX include:

   o **Ease of Navigation**: A well-structured navigation menu that makes it easy for users to find what they are looking for.

- o **Fast Load Times**: Websites that load quickly reduce bounce rates and improve user satisfaction.

- o **Clear Calls to Action (CTAs)**: Prominent and well-placed buttons or links that guide users to take desired actions, such as making a purchase or filling out a contact form.

- o **Mobile Responsiveness**: Ensuring that your website looks and functions well on mobile devices is critical in today's mobile-first world.

A website with great UX design helps ensure that users stay engaged, return to your site, and are more likely to take action, whether it's subscribing to a newsletter or completing a purchase.

2. **User Interface (UI):** UI, on the other hand, refers to the visual design and layout of your website. While UX focuses on the site's functionality and usability, UI deals with how the site looks and how design elements are presented to users. UI includes elements such as buttons, menus, fonts, colors, and images—

everything that users see and interact with on the website.

Key elements of good UI design include:

- **Consistency**: Using consistent fonts, colors, and design elements throughout the site helps create a cohesive and professional look.

- **Aesthetics**: A visually appealing design enhances user experience and encourages users to stay on the site longer.

- **Intuitive Layout**: A layout that organizes content logically and places important elements where users expect to find them.

Good UI design contributes to the overall user experience by making the site easy to use and visually attractive. A website with great UI design will catch the user's eye and encourage them to engage with your content.

To ensure your website's success, both UX and UI need to be optimized for ease of use, visual appeal, and seamless functionality. This requires careful planning and design, as well as attention to detail when choosing themes, layouts, and features.

Introduction to Page Builders: Elementor vs. Gutenberg

When it comes to designing your website in WordPress, page builders are essential tools that allow you to create stunning, customized pages without the need for any coding knowledge. WordPress provides two primary methods for building pages: the **Gutenberg block editor** (default) and **Elementor** (a popular page builder plugin). Each of these tools offers its own set of features, and choosing the right one depends on your specific needs and preferences.

1. **Gutenberg (Block Editor):** Gutenberg is WordPress's built-in block-based editor, introduced in WordPress 5.0. It replaces the classic editor and allows users to build pages and posts using blocks, which are modular units that can hold different types of content, such as text, images, videos, buttons, and more. Gutenberg's block system provides a clean, visual interface, making it easier for users to

organize content and customize the layout without using shortcodes or custom HTML.

Key features of Gutenberg include:

○ **Blocks for Content Creation**: Gutenberg comes with a wide variety of blocks that allow you to add different content elements, such as paragraphs, headings, images, buttons, lists, and galleries.

○ **Reusable Blocks**: If you create a block that you want to use across multiple pages or posts, you can save it as a reusable block and insert it wherever needed.

○ **Built-in Customization**: Gutenberg offers customization options for each block, allowing you to adjust margins, padding, colors, and fonts.

While Gutenberg is great for basic page design, it is limited compared to third-party page builders in terms of design flexibility and advanced features.

2. **Elementor:** Elementor is a drag-and-drop page builder plugin that offers more advanced design capabilities than the default Gutenberg editor. It allows users to build highly customized pages with precision, using a live editor to see changes in real-time. Elementor provides a wide range of widgets (such as text, images, forms, sliders, and social media icons) and customization options that allow you to create beautiful, professional-looking websites without writing any code.

Key features of Elementor include:

- o **Drag-and-Drop Editor**: Elementor's intuitive drag-and-drop interface makes it easy to create custom layouts without needing to code.

- o **Pre-designed Templates**: Elementor offers a library of pre-designed templates and blocks, which can be imported and customized to speed up the design process.

- o **Advanced Design Options**: With Elementor, you have full control over the spacing, typography, colors, and layout of every element on the page. It also includes advanced features such as animations, pop-ups, and dynamic content.

- o **Mobile Editing**: Elementor allows you to design and optimize pages specifically for mobile devices, ensuring that your site looks great on smartphones and tablets.

Elementor is widely regarded as one of the most powerful page builders available for WordPress. It is particularly useful for users who want to create highly customized, visually appealing websites. However, while Elementor offers extensive features, the sheer number of options and settings can also be overwhelming for beginners.

Creating Stunning Pages with Page Builders: A Step-by-Step Guide

Whether you use Gutenberg or Elementor, creating a stunning page involves understanding the layout, design, and features that best suit your website's purpose. Here's a step-by-step guide for both Gutenberg and Elementor to help you create stunning pages:

Using Gutenberg (Block Editor):

1. **Create a New Page:**

   o From your WordPress dashboard, navigate to **Pages** > **Add New**.

   o Give your page a title and click **Publish** to create the page.

2. **Add Blocks to Your Page:**

   o Gutenberg works by adding blocks to your page. To add a block, click on the + sign that appears when you hover over the content area.

   o Choose from a wide variety of blocks, including paragraphs, headings, images, galleries, buttons, and more. Each block can be customized individually by clicking on it and adjusting the settings in the sidebar.

3. **Arrange Blocks:**

- To arrange the blocks, drag and drop them into place. You can add multiple blocks in a row or stack them vertically, depending on the layout you want.

4. **Customize the Blocks:**

- Each block has its settings. For example, when you select an image block, you can adjust the image size, alignment, and add a link. Similarly, for text blocks, you can change the font, color, and style.

5. **Publish Your Page:**

- Once you're satisfied with the design, click **Publish** to make your page live.

Using Elementor:

1. **Install and Activate Elementor:**

- If you haven't already, go to **Plugins > Add New** in your dashboard and search for Elementor. Install and activate the plugin.

2. **Create a New Page:**

- Go to **Pages** > **Add New** and enter a title for your page.

- Click on the **Edit with Elementor** button to launch the Elementor editor.

3. **Choose a Template or Start from Scratch:**

- Elementor offers a variety of pre-designed templates, which you can import and modify. Alternatively, you can start with a blank canvas and design your page from scratch.

4. **Add Widgets and Customize:**

- On the left panel, you'll find a list of widgets such as text, images, buttons, headings, forms, and more. Drag the widget onto the page and adjust its settings on the left panel.

- You can customize each widget's layout, style, and advanced settings to match your desired design.

5. **Preview and Publish:**

o Once you're happy with your design, click the **Preview** button to see how your page looks. When you're ready, click **Publish** to make it live.

Customizing Your Homepage, About Page, and Contact Form

Your homepage, about page, and contact form are essential components of your website. These pages give visitors a first impression of your site and provide them with important information.

1. **Customizing the Homepage:** The homepage is often the first page visitors see when they come to your site, so it's important to make it visually appealing and easy to navigate. To customize your homepage, consider including the following elements:

   o **Hero Section**: A large, eye-catching image or video with a call to action (CTA) that directs visitors to your key offerings.

   o **Introduction**: A brief overview of who you are and what your website offers.

o **Featured Content**: Showcase your latest blog posts, products, or services to give visitors an idea of what they can expect from your site.

o **Navigation**: Ensure that the navigation menu is easy to find and intuitive, allowing users to access key areas of your site quickly.

2. **Customizing the About Page:** Your about page is an opportunity to tell your story, explain your mission, and connect with your audience. To create an engaging about page, consider including:

o **Your Story**: Share a brief history of your brand or website and why it matters.

o **Team Members**: If you have a team, introduce them with short bios and pictures.

o **Values and Mission**: Let visitors know what you stand for and what they can expect from your content or services.

3. **Customizing the Contact Form:** A contact form makes it easy for visitors to get in touch with you. Using Elementor or a plugin like WPForms, you can create a simple contact form with fields for name, email, message, and a submit button. To enhance the user experience, be sure to add a confirmation message or thank you note once the form is submitted.

Adding Media: Images, Videos, and Galleries

Media plays a significant role in website design. High-quality images, videos, and galleries can help tell your story, promote products, and enhance user engagement. WordPress makes it easy to add and manage media:

1. **Adding Images:**

   o Use the **Image** block in Gutenberg or the **Image** widget in Elementor to add images to your site.

   o Optimize images for fast loading by reducing file sizes without sacrificing quality.

2. **Adding Videos:**

   o Embed videos from platforms like YouTube or Vimeo by adding a **Video** block (Gutenberg) or **Video** widget (Elementor).

   o Alternatively, you can upload videos directly to your WordPress site using the media library.

3. **Adding Galleries:**

   o Both Gutenberg and Elementor allow you to create galleries of images that visitors can browse. You can use the **Gallery** block (Gutenberg) or the **Gallery** widget (Elementor) to display multiple images in a grid or lightbox format.

Creating and Managing a Blog

Blogging is a key component of many WordPress websites, allowing you to share content, engage with your audience, and improve SEO. To create and manage a blog on WordPress:

1. **Create Blog Posts:**

- Go to **Posts** > **Add New** to create a new blog post. Use Gutenberg or Elementor to format your post and add images, videos, and other media.

2. **Organize Blog Posts:**

   - Categorize and tag your blog posts to make it easier for visitors to find content related to specific topics. You can manage categories and tags directly from the **Posts** section.

3. **Display Blog Posts on the Homepage:**

   - Customize your homepage to display your most recent blog posts or create a dedicated blog page using either Gutenberg or Elementor.

Designing your website with WordPress is an exciting process that allows you to create a site that reflects your style, goals, and brand identity. By understanding UX and UI principles and using powerful design tools like Gutenberg and Elementor, you can create a visually appealing and functional site. Whether you're designing your homepage, about page, or contact form, customizing your site with media and a blog will enhance the user experience and provide valuable content for your audience.

Chapter 6: Content Creation and Management

Creating and managing content is one of the most important aspects of running a successful website. Whether you're blogging, sharing portfolio items, or running an online store, your content plays a crucial role in driving traffic, engaging your audience, and achieving your goals. In this chapter, we will guide you through the process of creating high-quality content for your website, share best practices for writing blog posts and articles, explain how to organize your content with categories and tags, and show you how to manage comments and user engagement. Additionally, we'll cover how to add and manage different types of content, such as posts, pages, and custom post types, to keep your website organized and dynamic.

How to Create High-Quality Content for Your Website

Creating high-quality content is essential for attracting visitors to your website and keeping them engaged. High-quality content should be informative, relevant, well-written, and easy to read. Here are some key steps to creating compelling content for your WordPress website:

1. **Understand Your Audience:** The first step to creating great content is understanding your audience. Who are they? What problems do they need solving? What type of content will resonate with them? Take the time to research your audience's preferences, interests, and pain points. Consider using tools like Google Analytics, social media insights, and surveys to gather data on your audience's demographics and behaviors.

2. **Focus on Value:** Your content should provide real value to your audience. This means offering solutions to their problems, answering their questions, and providing useful insights. Whether you're writing a blog post, creating a product description, or sharing an informational article, ensure that your content addresses your audience's needs. For example, if you're writing a blog post on "How to Improve Your SEO," make sure to offer practical tips and actionable advice rather than just generic information.

3. **Write with Clarity and Precision:** High-quality content is clear, concise, and easy to

understand. Avoid jargon, unnecessary technical terms, or overly complicated language that may confuse your readers. Instead, please write in a simple, straightforward style that makes it easy for your audience to follow along. Short paragraphs, bullet points, and subheadings are great tools for breaking up large blocks of text and improving readability.

4. **Optimize for SEO:** Search engine optimization (SEO) plays a critical role in how your content ranks in search engine results. To create SEO-friendly content, focus on incorporating relevant keywords naturally within your content. However, avoid keyword stuffing, which can negatively affect readability. Other important SEO practices include using proper heading tags (H1, H2, H3), optimizing images with descriptive alt text, and adding internal and external links where relevant.

5. **Engage with Compelling Headlines:** A great headline can make or break your content. A headline should be attention-grabbing and make the reader want to click on it. Use action verbs, ask questions, or address a pain point

your audience may have. For example, instead of "SEO Tips," a more engaging headline might be "5 SEO Tips That Will Boost Your Website's Ranking in 2025."

6. **Use Visuals to Complement Content:** People are naturally drawn to visuals, so including high-quality images, infographics, videos, or charts in your content can make it more engaging. Visuals not only break up text but also help clarify complex ideas and improve the overall user experience. Be sure to optimize your images for fast loading times and use captions that provide additional context.

7. **Maintain Consistency and Quality:** Consistency is key to building trust and engagement with your audience. Posting regularly and keeping the quality of your content high will encourage users to come back for more. Whether you are posting weekly blog articles or adding new product pages, ensure that your content is consistent in tone, style, and message.

Best Practices for Writing Blog Posts and Articles

Writing blog posts and articles requires a strategic approach to ensure they are engaging, informative, and easy to digest. Below are best practices to help you write high-quality blog posts and articles for your WordPress website:

1. **Start with a Strong Introduction:** Your introduction is the first impression readers will have of your content, so it's important to make it compelling. The introduction should quickly grab the reader's attention and give them a reason to continue reading. Start with a hook, such as a surprising fact, a question, or a bold statement, and then clearly outline what the article will cover.

2. **Break Content into Digestible Sections:** Long paragraphs can overwhelm readers and make your content difficult to read. To make your content more accessible, break it into smaller sections with clear subheadings. Each section should focus on one main idea, and subheadings should summarize the content to come, helping readers navigate the post easily.

3. **Use Bullet Points and Numbered Lists:** When listing tips, steps, or ideas, use bullet points or numbered lists. This helps to break up dense text and makes it easier for readers to scan the content. For example, if you're writing about "10 Ways to Improve Your Website's SEO," use a numbered list to present each tip clearly.

4. **Provide Clear, Actionable Takeaways:** Readers often want practical advice that they can apply immediately. Whenever possible, provide clear, actionable takeaways at the end of each post or article. Summarize the main points in a few bullet points or a concise paragraph, and provide additional resources for readers who want to learn more.

5. **Proofread and Edit:** Before publishing, always proofread your content to catch spelling, grammar, and punctuation errors. Editing is crucial for maintaining professionalism and readability. Use tools like Grammarly or Hemingway to improve your writing and make it more concise. Consider reading the article

aloud to identify awkward phrasing or sentence structure issues.

6. **Add a Call to Action (CTA):** At the end of every blog post or article, include a clear call to action (CTA). A CTA encourages the reader to take the next step, whether it's signing up for your newsletter, downloading an e-book, leaving a comment, or exploring related content. For example, "Sign up for our newsletter to receive weekly tips on improving your website's SEO."

Organizing Content with Categories and Tags

Organizing your content effectively is key to making your website user-friendly and helping visitors find what they're looking for. WordPress provides two primary tools for organizing content: categories and tags. Let's explore how to use these tools to manage your website's content:

1. **Categories:** Categories are broad groupings that help organize your content into general topics. For example, if you have a blog about digital marketing, you might use categories like

"SEO," "Social Media," "Email Marketing," and "Content Marketing." Categories are hierarchical, meaning you can have parent categories with subcategories beneath them.

Best practices for using categories:

- o Limit the number of categories to avoid overwhelming your audience.

- o Assign each post to only one or two categories to keep the site organized.

- o Use categories to help readers navigate your site and find related content easily.

2. **Tags:** Tags are more specific than categories and allow you to describe the details of a post. Tags are non-hierarchical, meaning they are not organized into broader groups. Tags help readers find more specific content related to certain topics or keywords. For example, a blog post about "SEO Tips" might have tags like "keyword research," "backlinks," or "on-page optimization."

Best practices for using tags:

- Use tags to focus on specific details or subtopics mentioned in the content.

- Avoid using too many tags—aim for 5 to 10 relevant tags per post.

- Keep your tags concise and descriptive.

By effectively using categories and tags, you can help users find content more easily and improve your site's SEO.

Managing Comments and User Engagement

Engaging with your audience is an important part of managing your WordPress site. Comments allow users to share their thoughts, ask questions, and interact with your content. Managing comments effectively can help foster a sense of community and increase user engagement. Here are some best practices for managing comments and fostering engagement on your site:

1. **Moderate Comments:** As a website owner, you can choose to moderate comments before they are published on your site. This is an essential step to prevent spam, inappropriate

content, or irrelevant comments from being posted. You can enable comment moderation under **Settings** > **Discussion** in your WordPress dashboard.

2. **Respond to Comments:** Engaging with your audience is key to building a loyal community. Responding to comments shows that you value your readers' feedback and encourages further interaction. When responding to comments, be respectful and thoughtful and try to add value to the conversation.

3. **Use Anti-Spam Plugins:** Spam comments can quickly flood your website, making it difficult for genuine comments to stand out. To prevent this, install an anti-spam plugin like **Akismet** or **Antispam Bee**. These plugins automatically filter out spammy comments, saving you time and effort.

4. **Encourage User-Generated Content:** Encourage your audience to participate in the conversation by asking questions or prompting them to leave their thoughts in the comments. You can also host user-generated content

contests or invite guest bloggers to contribute content. The more engagement you foster, the more likely your audience will return to your site regularly.

5. **Display Recent Comments:** Consider displaying recent comments on your blog sidebar or footer. This allows new visitors to see the ongoing discussions and may encourage them to join the conversation.

How to Add and Manage Different Types of Content: Posts, Pages, Custom Post Types

WordPress allows you to add and manage different types of content, including posts, pages, and custom post types. Each type of content serves a specific purpose, and knowing how to manage them effectively is crucial for running a well-organized website.

1. **Posts:** Posts are typically used for blog content and are displayed in reverse chronological order on your site. Posts are often used for news articles, tutorials, opinion pieces, and other types of time-sensitive content. Posts are

categorized and tagged, and they are often organized into archives based on publication dates.

To add a new post:

- o Go to **Posts** > **Add New**.

- o Enter your post title and content in the editor.

- o Assign categories and tags.

- o Click **Publish** when you are ready to make the post live.

2. **Pages:** Pages are static content typically used for essential information on your website, such as your homepage, about page, contact page, and privacy policy. Categories or tags do not organize them and are typically displayed in the main navigation menu.

To add a new page:

- o Go to **Pages** > **Add New**.

- o Enter your page title and content.

- o Click **Publish** to make the page live.

3. **Custom Post Types:** Custom post types allow you to create specialized content beyond posts and pages. For example, if you run an online store, you may create a custom post type for products. If you run a portfolio site, you might create a custom post type for portfolio items. Custom post types can be customized with unique fields, taxonomies, and templates.

To add a custom post type, you will need to either use a plugin (such as Custom Post Type UI) or add custom code to your theme's functions.php file.

Managing content effectively is key to running a successful WordPress website. By creating high-quality, engaging content and organizing it with categories and tags, you can ensure that your visitors find the information they are looking for. Effective comment management and user engagement can help foster a sense of community, while understanding how to use posts, pages, and custom post types will keep your site organized and dynamic. Follow the best practices outlined in this chapter to enhance your content creation and management strategy.

Chapter 7: Optimizing Your Website for SEO

Search engine optimization (SEO) is an essential practice for improving the visibility of your website in search engine results, driving organic traffic, and ultimately achieving your business or personal goals. Without proper SEO, your website might get lost in the vast sea of online content. Fortunately, WordPress, with its range of plugins and tools, makes SEO implementation accessible to users of all levels. In this chapter, we will walk you through basic SEO principles for WordPress websites, show you how to use SEO plugins to optimize your content, explain the importance of title tags, meta descriptions, and keywords, and guide you on how to improve your website's speed and performance for better SEO. We'll also cover how to create XML sitemaps and submit them to search engines, as well as how to build backlinks and improve on-page SEO.

Basic SEO Principles for WordPress Websites

Before diving into specific tools and techniques, it's important to understand the fundamental SEO principles that underpin successful optimization efforts. SEO involves multiple components, each contributing to a website's ranking in search engine results. Here are the key SEO principles you need to know:

1. **Keyword Research**: Keywords are the words and phrases that users type into search engines when looking for information. Effective keyword research allows you to target the right terms that your audience is searching for. By optimizing your content with relevant keywords, you can increase the likelihood of your website appearing in search results. Keyword research tools such as Google Keyword Planner, Ubersuggest, and SEMrush can help you discover keywords that are highly relevant to your website's content.

   o **Primary Keywords**: These are the main terms that you want your page to rank for.

   o **Secondary Keywords**: These are related terms that also help optimize your content but aren't the primary focus.

- Long-tail Keywords: These are more specific, longer phrases that are typically less competitive but have a higher conversion rate.

2. **On-Page SEO**: On-page SEO refers to optimizing individual web pages to rank higher in search engines and drive more relevant traffic. It includes elements such as title tags, meta descriptions, URL structure, headers, images, and internal links. On-page SEO is one of the most effective ways to improve search engine rankings, as it directly impacts how search engines understand your content.

Key on-page SEO elements include:

- **Title Tags**: Title tags are one of the most important on-page SEO factors. They provide search engines and users with a concise idea of what the page is about.

- **Meta Descriptions**: Meta descriptions provide a brief summary of your page and often appear below the title tag in search results.

o **Headings**: Using proper heading tags (H1, H2, H3) helps structure your content and makes it easier for both users and search engines to understand the page's topic.

o **Image Optimization**: Including optimized images with descriptive alt text can help improve rankings and ensure that your content is accessible to all users.

o **Internal Linking**: Linking to other pages or posts on your site helps search engines crawl your site and can improve your site's SEO.

3. **Off-Page SEO**: Off-page SEO refers to actions taken outside of your website to improve its ranking. The most important off-page SEO element is **backlinks**—links from other websites that point to your content. Backlinks act as "votes of confidence" for your content, signaling to search engines that your website is credible and authoritative. The more high-

quality backlinks your website has, the higher it will rank in search results.

4. **Mobile Optimization**: With more users browsing the internet on mobile devices than ever before, mobile optimization has become a critical factor in SEO. Google uses mobile-first indexing, meaning it primarily uses the mobile version of your site for indexing and ranking. If your website is not mobile-friendly, it may be penalized in search rankings. Ensure your website is responsive and provides an optimal experience for users on smartphones and tablets.

5. **Site Speed and Performance**: Website speed is an important ranking factor for SEO. A slow website can negatively impact user experience, increase bounce rates, and lower rankings in search engine results. Optimizing your site's speed through techniques like image compression, caching, and code minification is essential for both SEO and user satisfaction.

6. **Content Quality**: Content is one of the most important ranking factors for SEO. High-quality

content that provides value to users is more likely to rank higher in search results. Focus on creating informative, engaging, and well-researched content that answers the questions your audience is searching for. Long-form content tends to perform better in search results, but it must be relevant, well-written, and offer valuable insights.

How to Use SEO Plugins to Optimize Your Content

WordPress offers a range of SEO plugins that make it easier for website owners to implement SEO best practices. These plugins can automate and streamline many aspects of SEO, saving you time while helping your website rank better in search engine results. The most popular SEO plugin for WordPress is **Yoast SEO**, but there are other options like **Rank Math** and **All in One SEO Pack**.

Here's how to use Yoast SEO (one of the most popular SEO plugins for WordPress) to optimize your content:

1. **Installing Yoast SEO**:

   o Go to your WordPress dashboard and navigate to **Plugins** > **Add New**.

- Search for **Yoast SEO** and click **Install Now**.

- After the installation is complete, click **Activate**.

2. **Configuring Yoast SEO**: After activation, Yoast SEO will guide you through a simple configuration process. This includes setting up basic settings, such as whether your site is a personal blog or a business site, and configuring social media profiles and webmaster tools.

3. **Optimizing Content with Yoast SEO**:

   - **Focus Keyword**: In the Yoast SEO meta box, you'll see a field to enter your focus keyword. This is the primary keyword you want the page to rank for. Yoast will then analyze your content and give you suggestions on how to improve keyword usage throughout the page.

   - **SEO Title**: The SEO title is the title that appears in search engine results. Yoast allows you to customize this title to make it more enticing and relevant to your target keyword.

- o **Meta Description**: The meta description is a summary of the content that appears beneath the title in search results. Yoast provides a space to write a compelling meta description that includes your target keyword.

- o **Readability**: Yoast SEO also provides a readability analysis that checks the structure of your content, including sentence length, paragraph structure, and use of transition words. Ensuring that your content is easy to read is crucial for both user engagement and SEO.

- o **Internal Linking**: Yoast SEO suggests adding internal links to relevant pages or posts on your website, improving navigation and spreading link equity throughout your site.

Yoast SEO provides a comprehensive and user-friendly way to optimize your content for search engines. It ensures that your pages are properly optimized and more likely to rank higher.

The Importance of Title Tags, Meta Descriptions, and Keywords

Title tags, meta descriptions, and keywords are foundational elements of on-page SEO that play a critical role in improving your site's visibility and click-through rates in search results.

1. **Title Tags**: The title tag is one of the most important SEO elements because it tells both users and search engines what the page is about. Title tags are displayed in search engine results and the browser tab when someone visits your site.

Best practices for title tags:

- o Keep the title under 60 characters to ensure it doesn't get cut off in search results.

- o Include your target keyword near the beginning of the title.

- o Make the title enticing and relevant to the content to encourage clicks.

- o Avoid keyword stuffing—make sure the title reads naturally.

2. **Meta Descriptions**: The meta description is a summary (usually around 150-160 characters) of your content that appears beneath the title in search results. While meta descriptions do not directly affect rankings, they play a significant role in click-through rates (CTR). A compelling meta description can increase the likelihood that users will click on your page.

Best practices for meta descriptions:

- o Write clear, concise summaries that accurately describe the page's content.

- o Include your target keyword, but don't over-optimize.

- o Make it actionable—use verbs that encourage users to click, such as "learn," "discover," or "find out."

- o Avoid duplicate meta descriptions across your website.

3. **Keywords**: Keywords are the terms and phrases your audience is searching for, and

optimizing your content for these keywords is a key aspect of SEO. It's important to use relevant keywords naturally in your content, including in titles, headings, and throughout the body text.

Best practices for keyword optimization:

- Focus on long-tail keywords, which are less competitive and more likely to convert.

- Use your primary keyword in the title, URL, and meta description.

- Incorporate related keywords and variations of your target keyword to improve content relevance and avoid keyword stuffing.

- Use keyword research tools to identify the best keywords for your content.

How to Improve Website Speed and Performance for Better SEO

Website speed is a critical factor in both user experience and SEO. Slow websites can lead to higher bounce rates, lower user engagement, and poor rankings in search engine results. Fortunately, there are several techniques you can use to improve your website's speed and performance.

1. **Optimize Images**: Large images can significantly slow down your website. To improve page load times, use image compression tools like **Smush** or **Imagify** to reduce image file sizes without sacrificing quality.

2. **Enable Caching**: Caching stores copies of your site's pages and posts in the user's browser, so they don't have to be reloaded every time a visitor accesses your site. Using a caching plugin like **WP Super Cache** or **W3 Total Cache** can improve page load times by serving cached versions of your pages.

3. **Minify CSS, JavaScript, and HTML**: Minifying these files removes unnecessary spaces, comments, and characters, making them smaller and faster to load. Plugins like **Autoptimize** can help you minify your site's code.

4. **Use a Content Delivery Network (CDN)**: A CDN distributes your website's static files (such as images, JavaScript, and CSS) across multiple servers around the world, allowing visitors to download them from a server closer to their location. Services like **Cloudflare** or **KeyCDN** can help speed up your website.

5. **Choose a Reliable Hosting Provider**: Your hosting provider plays a significant role in your website's speed. Choose a hosting provider with a reputation for fast, reliable service. Consider upgrading to **VPS hosting** or **managed WordPress hosting** if you're currently using shared hosting.

Creating XML Sitemaps and Submitting to Search Engines

An XML sitemap is a file that lists all the important pages of your website, helping search engines crawl and index your site more efficiently. By submitting your sitemap to search engines like Google and Bing, you ensure that they can discover and index your content more quickly.

1. **Create an XML Sitemap**:

o Yoast SEO automatically generates an XML sitemap for your website. To find it, go to **SEO > General > Features** and make sure the "XML Sitemaps" option is enabled.

o Alternatively, you can use plugins like **Google XML Sitemaps** to generate a sitemap manually.

2. **Submit Your Sitemap to Google**:

o To submit your sitemap to Google, log in to Google Search Console, navigate to the **Sitemaps** section, and enter the URL of your sitemap (usually yourdomain.com/sitemap_index.xml).

o Click **Submit** to let Google know that your sitemap is available.

3. **Submit to Bing**:

o Similarly, you can submit your sitemap to Bing through **Bing Webmaster Tools**.

Building Backlinks and Improving On-Page SEO

Backlinks are one of the most important off-page SEO factors. They act as "votes of confidence" for your content, signaling to search engines that your website is credible and authoritative.

1. **Build Backlinks**:

   o Focus on earning high-quality backlinks from reputable sites in your niche. Write guest posts, participate in industry forums, and reach out to influencers for collaboration opportunities.

   o Avoid low-quality, spammy backlinks that can harm your site's reputation.

2. **Improve On-Page SEO**:

   o Use proper heading tags (H1, H2, H3) to structure your content and make it easier for search engines to understand.

   o Add internal links to connect related content on your site and help users find more relevant information.

- Optimize images with descriptive alt text, which helps search engines understand the content of the images.

SEO is an ongoing process, but by implementing the strategies discussed in this chapter, you can significantly improve your website's visibility and performance. From keyword optimization and title tags to improving site speed and building backlinks, the right SEO practices will help your website achieve higher rankings in search engine results and attract more organic traffic. With tools like Yoast SEO and proper optimization techniques, you can ensure that your WordPress website is well-optimized and ready to rank.

Chapter 8: E-Commerce with WordPress – Setting Up an Online Store

WordPress is not just a blogging platform; it's also a powerful tool for creating fully functional e-commerce websites. One of the most popular ways to set up an online store with WordPress is through the **WooCommerce** plugin. WooCommerce is a feature-rich and highly customizable e-commerce solution that integrates seamlessly with WordPress, enabling you to sell physical and digital products, manage inventory, process payments, and much more. In this chapter, we will walk you through the process of setting up WooCommerce, configuring payment gateways, adding products, customizing your shop and checkout pages, managing orders and shipping settings, and optimizing your e-commerce site for better visibility.

Introduction to WooCommerce: The E-Commerce Plugin for WordPress

WooCommerce is a free WordPress plugin that transforms a WordPress website into a fully functional e-commerce store. Originally launched in 2011, It has grown into one of the most widely used e-commerce platforms, powering millions of online stores worldwide. It is open-source and highly customizable, meaning you can tailor your store to meet your unique business needs.

WooCommerce enables you to sell a wide range of products, including physical items, digital downloads, and even subscriptions. It provides all the essential features for running an online store, such as product management, order processing, payment integration, and customer management. Furthermore, WooCommerce supports an extensive range of third-party extensions and themes, which makes it easy to add extra functionality, such as enhanced shipping options, advanced payment gateways, and marketing tools.

What makes WooCommerce especially attractive is its tight integration with WordPress. Since WordPress is one of the most popular content management systems (CMS), you can take advantage of all the tools, themes, and plugins WordPress offers, making it an ideal solution for building a fully functional e-commerce site.

Setting Up WooCommerce and Configuring Payment Gateways

The first step in setting up your online store is to install and configure the WooCommerce plugin. Fortunately, WooCommerce is very easy to install, and WordPress makes the process even simpler.

Installing WooCommerce

1. **Install the Plugin**:

    o   In your WordPress dashboard, go to **Plugins > Add New**.

    o   Search for **WooCommerce** in the search bar and click **Install Now**.

    o   Once the plugin is installed, click **Activate**.

2. **WooCommerce Setup Wizard**: After activating WooCommerce, you will be prompted to run the WooCommerce Setup Wizard. This is an automated process that will guide you through the initial setup of your store. The wizard includes essential configuration steps, such as:

- o Setting your store's location and currency

- o Configuring tax settings (e.g., whether you charge taxes on products)

- o Choosing your preferred payment methods

- o Setting up shipping options (more on this later)

The WooCommerce Setup Wizard is an excellent starting point for beginners, and it will help you set up your store quickly. However, if you want to fine-tune your settings further, you can always go to the WooCommerce settings section under **WooCommerce > Settings**.

Configuring Payment Gateways

WooCommerce supports a wide variety of payment gateways, allowing you to accept payments from customers worldwide. Payment gateways are third-party services that process payments securely, enabling customers to pay for their orders.

1. **WooCommerce Built-In Payment Options**: WooCommerce comes with built-in support for several popular payment gateways, including:

   o **PayPal**: One of the most widely used payment methods for online transactions.

   o **Stripe**: A payment gateway that allows you to accept credit and debit card payments directly on your site.

   o **Bank Transfer**: You can also accept payments via direct bank transfers.

   o **Cash on Delivery (COD)**: This is an option where customers pay for the order when it is delivered.

2. **Adding New Payment Gateways**:

   o To configure these gateways, navigate to **WooCommerce > Settings > Payments**.

   o You will see a list of available payment options. Click **Set up** next to the payment method you wish to enable (e.g., PayPal or Stripe).

- o Follow the on-screen instructions to connect your payment gateway account with your WooCommerce store.

3. **Third-Party Payment Gateways**: If you want to offer additional payment options, WooCommerce has many third-party extensions for gateways like **Authorize.net**, **Square**, and **Klarna**. These extensions can be installed just like any other WordPress plugin, and they often come with their configuration settings.

4. **Testing Payment Gateways**: After setting up your payment gateways, it's essential to test them to make sure they are functioning properly. You can do this by making a test purchase, checking if payments are processed, and verifying that you receive payment notifications.

Adding Products and Managing Inventory

Once you have WooCommerce set up and payment gateways configured, the next step is to add products to your store and manage your inventory. WooCommerce allows you to sell a variety of products, including simple products, variable products (with different sizes or colors), downloadable products (like software or eBooks), and even virtual products (such as services).

Adding Simple Products

To add a simple product to your store:

1. Navigate to **Products > Add New**.

2. Enter the product name and description.

3. Set the **Product Data** section:

    o   Select **Simple product** if you're selling a single, standalone item.

    o   Enter the price, SKU (stock-keeping unit), and other details.

    o   You can also set product visibility, tax status, and shipping options.

4. Under the Product Image section, add product images, such as the main product image and gallery images.

5. Select relevant **Product Categories** and add **Tags** if desired to help customers find your product.

6. Click **Publish** to make the product live on your site.

Adding Variable Products

You can create a variable product if your product has multiple variations (e.g., different sizes or colors).

1. Under **Product Data**, select **Variable product** from the dropdown menu.

2. Navigate to the **Attributes** tab, and add the attributes (such as size, color, etc.).

3. Under the **Variations** tab, configure each variation with its price, SKU, stock level, and image.

Managing Inventory

WooCommerce allows you to manage your product inventory directly from the product page. You can enable stock management, set stock quantities, and receive notifications when stock is running low. Here's how to manage inventory:

1. Go to **Products** > **All Products** and select the product you want to edit.

2. In the **Product Data** section, navigate to the **Inventory** tab.

3. Enable **Manage Stock** and enter the stock quantity.

4. Set **Stock Status** to "In Stock," "Out of Stock," or "On Backorder."

5. For variable products, you can set stock for each variation individually.

Customizing the Shop Page, Cart, and Checkout Pages

Your shop page, cart, and checkout pages are essential components of your online store. Customizing these pages can enhance the user experience, improve conversions, and create a more cohesive brand experience.

Customizing the Shop Page

By default, WooCommerce creates a shop page that displays all of your products. However, you can customize the layout and appearance of the shop page using the following methods:

1. **Using the WordPress Customizer**:

    o Navigate to **Appearance** > **Customize** > **WooCommerce** > **Product Catalog**.

    o Here, you can control the default product sorting options (e.g., by price or popularity), how products are displayed (grid or list), and the number of products per page.

2. **Using a Page Builder (e.g., Elementor)**:

    o If you want more control over the layout, you can use a page builder like **Elementor** to design your shop page. Elementor allows you to drag and drop elements, such as product grids, product categories, and filters, to create a custom shop page.

3. **Customizing Product Displays**:

o   Customize how your products are
    displayed by modifying the
    WooCommerce product archive pages
    with templates or custom code. This will
    allow you to change how product titles,
    prices, and images are presented.

Customizing the Cart and Checkout Pages

Customers complete their purchases on the cart and checkout pages, so it's essential to make them as user-friendly as possible. WooCommerce provides default templates for these pages, but you can customize them to improve usability.

1.   **Using the WooCommerce Settings**:

     o   Go to **WooCommerce > Settings >
         Checkout** to configure settings such as
         which fields appear during checkout
         (e.g., billing, shipping, payment options)
         and whether the checkout process is
         simplified or includes multiple steps.

     o   You can enable guest checkout, which
         allows customers to make purchases
         without creating an account, or force

customers to create an account during checkout.

2. **Customizing Checkout Fields**:

   o You can use plugins like **Checkout Field Editor for WooCommerce** to add custom fields to the checkout page, such as gift messages, special instructions, or additional contact details.

3. **Styling with a Page Builder**:

   o If you are using a page builder like Elementor, you can further customize the cart and checkout pages by using the available widgets and layout options for WooCommerce. Some page builders offer dedicated WooCommerce widgets for cart and checkout pages, enabling you to design them according to your needs.

Managing Customer Orders and Shipping Settings

Once customers place orders, you need to manage and fulfill them efficiently. WooCommerce provides robust tools for tracking orders, managing customer information, and handling shipping.

Managing Orders

To view and manage customer orders:

1. Go to **WooCommerce** > **Orders**.

2. Here, you can view all the orders placed on your site. Orders are displayed with details such as order number, customer name, status, and total.

3. Click on any order to view the full order details, including product information, shipping address, payment method, and order status.

4. You can update the order status (e.g., processing, completed, canceled) and add notes for both the customer and your team.

Shipping Settings

WooCommerce offers several options for configuring shipping settings, including flat-rate shipping, free shipping, and real-time shipping quotes from carriers like UPS, FedEx, and USPS.

1. Go to **WooCommerce** > **Settings** > **Shipping**.

2. Add shipping zones based on the countries or regions you deliver to.

3. Set up shipping methods, such as:

    o **Flat Rate Shipping**: Charge a fixed amount per order, per item, or class.

    o **Free Shipping**: Offer free shipping based on conditions, such as minimum order value or use of a coupon code.

    o **Local Pickup**: Allow customers to pick up their orders in person.

You can also install extensions to integrate with third-party shipping providers or get real-time shipping rates based on the customer's location.

Basic E-Commerce SEO for Better Visibility

SEO is just as important for e-commerce sites as it is for blogs or informational websites. Optimizing your e-commerce site for search engines can help improve its visibility, attract more visitors, and increase sales.

1. **Optimize Product Pages**:

- o Use SEO-friendly URLs for your product pages, such as www.yoursite.com/product/product-name.

- o Write unique, compelling product descriptions that include relevant keywords.

- o Optimize product images with descriptive alt text to improve search engine visibility.

- o Include customer reviews on product pages, as reviews can help improve trust and encourage conversions.

2. **Use Structured Data (Schema Markup):**

- o Structured data helps search engines understand your content better. By adding schema markup to your product pages, you can display rich snippets in search results, such as product ratings, prices, and availability.

3. **Optimize for Mobile:**

- o Ensure that your website is mobile-friendly, as mobile traffic is growing rapidly. A responsive design will improve both user experience and SEO.

4. **Improve Site Speed**:

- o Fast-loading pages are critical for SEO. Use caching plugins, optimize images, and minimize code to improve site performance.

By following the steps outlined in this chapter, you can successfully set up an online store with WooCommerce and optimize it for both user experience and SEO. From configuring payment gateways and managing inventory to customizing your shop pages and optimizing product listings, WooCommerce provides all the tools you need to create and run a thriving e-commerce business. Whether you are just starting or looking to improve your existing store, WooCommerce offers the flexibility and power to grow your online business.

Chapter 9: Advanced Customization Techniques

When building a WordPress website, customization is one of the most powerful aspects of the platform. WordPress allows for a high degree of flexibility, but to take full advantage of its capabilities, it is essential to understand the basics of web development languages like HTML, CSS, and PHP. These are the building blocks of WordPress, and mastering them enables you to create truly unique websites that cater to your specific needs. In this chapter, we will explore advanced customization techniques for WordPress, covering essential topics such as understanding HTML, CSS, and PHP, customizing your theme's code safely, using child themes, creating custom page templates, integrating third-party services and APIs, and working with advanced custom fields and custom post types. These techniques will help you take your WordPress website to the next level, making it more dynamic, functional, and tailored to your specific requirements.

Understanding HTML, CSS, and PHP in WordPress

To get the most out of WordPress, it's essential to have a basic understanding of HTML, CSS, and PHP, as they are the core technologies used to build and style WordPress themes and customize its functionality. Here's a brief overview of each:

HTML (Hypertext Markup Language)

HTML is the fundamental language used to structure content on the web. It defines the elements on a webpage, such as headings, paragraphs, images, links, and more. HTML is made up of elements called **tags** that wrap around content to give it meaning and structure. WordPress themes are made up of HTML, and understanding it is essential if you want to modify your theme's structure or add custom content.

In WordPress, HTML is used primarily in the theme's templates (files like header.php, footer.php, single.php, etc.). These templates dictate how the content is displayed on your website. By editing these templates, you can customize the layout and appearance of your website.

CSS (Cascading Style Sheets)

CSS is used to control the visual appearance of HTML elements. It defines the layout, colors, fonts, spacing, and overall look of a website. While HTML structures the content, CSS styles that content to make it visually appealing. In WordPress, CSS is often used to customize the appearance of themes, change typography, modify colors, and adjust layouts.

CSS is usually found in the theme's style.css file, but it can also be added to individual pages or posts through the WordPress Customizer or additional CSS plugins. By modifying CSS, you can create custom styles that match your brand or personal preferences without altering the core structure of your WordPress theme.

PHP (Hypertext Preprocessor)

PHP is a server-side scripting language that powers WordPress and allows dynamic content to be displayed. Unlike HTML and CSS, which are static, PHP enables WordPress to fetch data from its database and display content on the page in real time. PHP is used to build WordPress themes, plugins, and functionality, and understanding it is essential if you want to customize WordPress beyond the appearance.

In WordPress, PHP is used in theme files (like index.php, functions.php, and others) to control dynamic content. PHP functions enable WordPress to generate content, handle form submissions, retrieve posts from the database, and manage various other aspects of your site.

Together, HTML, CSS, and PHP form the backbone of WordPress customization. While HTML and CSS handle structure and styling, PHP makes WordPress dynamic, allowing it to display data from your site's database and interact with users.

How to Customize Your Theme's Code (Without Breaking the Site)

Customizing your theme's code can seem daunting, but with the right approach, it's a relatively straightforward process. Here's how to safely modify your theme's code without breaking your website:

1. **Understand What You're Changing**: Before you start modifying theme files, it's crucial to understand the purpose of each file and what changes you are making. WordPress themes are made up of several template files,

including header.php, footer.php, single.php, index.php, and functions.php. Each of these files controls a specific aspect of your website's layout and functionality.

- o header.php: Contains the opening HTML structure, the site's logo, navigation menus, and metadata.

- o footer.php: Contains the closing HTML structure and footer content.

- o functions.php: Used for defining custom functions, hooks, and theme settings.

- o single.php: Used to display individual blog posts.

Before modifying these files, take time to familiarize yourself with their structure and function. This will help you understand how your changes affect the website.

2. **Backup Your Site**: Before making any changes to your theme's code, always create a full backup of your website. This includes backing up both the database and all the theme files. WordPress plugins like **UpdraftPlus** or

BackupBuddy can automate this process, ensuring that you can restore your site if something goes wrong.

3. **Use a Child Theme**: A child theme allows you to make customizations without altering the original theme's code directly. When you modify the code of a parent theme, your changes may be lost when the theme is updated. Using a child theme ensures that your customizations remain intact even after updates.

4. **Edit Theme Files Safely**: If you need to make changes to your theme's code, always do it through the WordPress theme editor or by accessing the files directly via FTP. Avoid editing files directly through the WordPress dashboard unless you are confident in your coding skills. Alternatively, you can use a code editor like **Sublime Text** or **Visual Studio Code** to make changes locally and then upload them to your server.

5. **Test Changes Locally**: If you have a local development environment set up (using software like **Local by Flywheel** or **XAMPP**),

you can make changes and test them without affecting the live website. This allows you to catch errors before they go public.

6. **Use the WordPress Customizer for CSS**: If you're only making style changes (e.g., changing colors or fonts), use the WordPress Customizer's **Additional CSS** section. This lets you add custom CSS without touching your theme's core files. To access this, go to **Appearance** > **Customize** > **Additional CSS**.

By following these practices, you can safely customize your WordPress theme and avoid common mistakes that could break your site.

Child Themes: Benefits of Overriding Theme Files Safely

Child themes are one of the most powerful tools available to WordPress users who want to customize their site without risking losing customizations after theme updates. A child theme is essentially a theme that inherits the functionality of a parent theme but allows you to override specific files or add custom functionality.

What is a Child Theme?

A child theme consists of two essential files:

1. **style.css**: This file is where you define the theme's metadata (such as the theme name, description, and version) and where you can add custom styles to override the parent theme's styles.

2. **functions.php**: This file is where you can add custom functions or modify existing functionality. It also allows you to include the parent theme's functions without altering the original theme files.

A child theme relies on the parent theme for the majority of its functionality and design, but you can customize it by adding or modifying files as needed.

Benefits of Using a Child Theme

1. **Preserve Customizations After Updates**: The primary benefit of using a child theme is that it preserves your customizations even when the parent theme is updated. WordPress will not overwrite your child theme's files during an

update, ensuring that your modifications remain intact.

2. **Safe Customization**: With a child theme, you can safely make changes to your theme's structure or style without fear of breaking the parent theme. If you make a mistake, you can simply revert to the parent theme's default settings.

3. **Easier Maintenance**: A child theme makes it easier to maintain and troubleshoot your customizations. You can clearly separate custom code from the default code, making it easier to identify and address issues.

4. **Enhanced Flexibility**: Child themes allow you to override specific parts of your theme (e.g., templates, styles) while leaving other parts untouched. This gives you greater flexibility and control over your site's design and functionality.

Creating a Child Theme

Creating a child theme is relatively simple. Here are the steps to create a basic child theme:

1. **Create a Child Theme Folder**: In the wp-content/themes directory, create a new folder for your child theme. Name it something like yourtheme-child.

2. **Create the style.css File**: In your child theme folder, create a file named style.css. This file should include the following header:

```css
CSS

/*
Theme Name: Your Theme Child
Template: yourtheme
*/
```

Replace yourtheme with the folder name of the parent theme. You can also add custom CSS below the header to override the parent theme's styles.

3. **Create the functions.php File**: In your child theme folder, create a functions.php file. This file should include the following code to enqueue the parent theme's styles:

Php

```php
<?php
function my_theme_enqueue_styles() {
    wp_enqueue_style('parent-style', get_template_directory_uri() . '/style.css');
}
add_action('wp_enqueue_scripts', 'my_theme_enqueue_styles');
```

4. **Activate Your Child Theme**: Once you've created your child theme folder and added the necessary files, go to your WordPress dashboard and navigate to **Appearance** > **Themes**. You should see your child theme listed there. Click **Activate** to use your child theme.

Creating Custom Page Templates and Layout Options

WordPress allows you to create custom page templates, which give you complete control over how specific pages are displayed. This is particularly useful when you want a unique layout for a specific page, such as a landing page, contact page, or custom portfolio page.

Creating a Custom Page Template

To create a custom page template:

1. **Create a New PHP File**: In your theme's folder (or child theme folder), create a new PHP file (e.g., custom-page.php).

2. **Add Template Header**: At the top of the new PHP file, add the following template header:

```php
<?php
/* Template Name: Custom Page Template */
?>
```

1. **Customize the Template**: Below the header, add the HTML, PHP, and WordPress template tags necessary to display your custom layout. You can add loops to display posts, static content, or even custom fields.

2. **Apply the Template**: Once you've created the custom page template, go to the WordPress dashboard and edit the page on which you want to use the template. In the **Page Attributes** section, you'll see a dropdown menu labeled **Template**. Select your custom template and click **Update**.

Customizing Layouts with Custom Fields

Custom fields allow you to add additional data to your pages or posts, such as a custom subtitle, image, or button text. They can also be used to customize layouts and add dynamic content.

1. **Enable Custom Fields**: If custom fields are not visible in the post or page editor, click on **Screen Options** at the top-right corner of the editor and check the box for **Custom Fields**.

2. **Add Custom Fields**: Below the content editor, you'll see a section to add custom fields. Please enter a name for the field and its value. For example, you could add a custom field called subtitle and assign it a value like "Welcome to My Store."

3. **Display Custom Fields in Templates**: To display custom fields on the front-end, use the get_post_meta() function in your theme templates. For example:

```php
$subtitle = get_post_meta($post->ID, 'subtitle', true);
echo '<h2>' . esc_html($subtitle) . '</h2>';
```

Integrating Third-Party Services and APIs with WordPress

WordPress can be extended with third-party services and APIs to add functionality such as payment processing, email marketing, or social media sharing. Integrating APIs allows you to connect WordPress with external services to enhance your site's capabilities.

Common API Integrations:

- **Payment Gateways**: Integrating payment gateways like **PayPal** or **Stripe** allows you to process payments securely and directly on your site.

- **Email Marketing Services**: Integrating services like **Mailchimp** or **Constant Contact** helps you manage email lists, send newsletters, and automate marketing campaigns.

- **Social Media**: Plugins like **Social Media Auto Publish** or **Instagram Feed** can integrate your site with social media platforms and automatically share content.

To integrate an API, you generally need to:

1. **Obtain an API Key**: Sign up for the service and get an API key or access token.

2. **Install a Plugin or Write Custom Code**: Some services provide official WordPress plugins, or you may need to write custom PHP code to interact with the API.

Introduction to Advanced Custom Fields and Custom Post Types

Advanced Custom Fields (ACF) is a powerful plugin that allows you to add custom fields to your posts, pages, and custom post types. This enables you to add extra information to your content, such as product details, testimonials, or events.

Custom Post Types (CPTs):

Custom post types are content types that go beyond the default WordPress posts and pages. For example, if you are building a portfolio, you could create a custom post type called "Portfolio" to organize your work better.

To create a custom post type, you can use the register_post_type() function or use a plugin like **Custom Post Type UI** to make the process easier.

Mastering these advanced customization techniques gives you full control over your WordPress website, enabling you to create truly unique and functional websites tailored to your needs. Whether you're using HTML, CSS, and PHP to modify your theme, creating custom page templates, or integrating third-party APIs, the possibilities for customization are vast. By following best practices and using tools like child themes, custom post types, and advanced custom fields, you can create a website that not only looks great but also provides a seamless user experience and powerful functionality.

Chapter 10: Security, Backup, and Maintenance

Website security, regular backups, and ongoing maintenance are fundamental to keeping your WordPress site running smoothly and ensuring it remains accessible, safe, and performant. WordPress, while a powerful platform, is vulnerable to a variety of online threats, ranging from hacking attempts to malware and even server failures. Without proper security measures, your site is at risk of being compromised, which could result in the loss of data, harm to your reputation, and even the complete shutdown of your website. Additionally, regular backups and site maintenance are necessary to prevent disruptions, ensure data safety, and keep your site optimized for performance. In this chapter, we will explore why website security is essential, best practices for securing your WordPress site, how to install and configure security plugins, how to back up your site regularly, and how to perform ongoing maintenance tasks to ensure the optimal performance and security of your website.

Why Website Security Matters and How to Secure Your WordPress Site

Website security is critical for protecting your WordPress site from a wide range of online threats, including hacking, malware, brute force attacks, and data theft. Cybercriminals are constantly finding new ways to exploit vulnerabilities in websites, and WordPress, being the most widely used content management system (CMS), is a prime target. A security breach can lead to the loss of valuable data, damage your website's reputation, and potentially result in significant financial losses if sensitive customer information is compromised.

Why Website Security Matters

1. **Protect Sensitive Data**: Websites often store sensitive data, such as customer personal information, payment details, and login credentials. A breach can expose this information to unauthorized individuals, leading to identity theft, financial fraud, or worse.

2. **Preserve Your Reputation**: A hacked website can quickly tarnish your reputation. Customers and visitors may lose trust in your ability to secure their data, leading to a decline in business. Even if you quickly recover, the long-term damage to your brand can be significant.

3. **Prevent Downtime**: Cyber-attacks, such as Distributed Denial of Service (DDoS) attacks, can bring your website down, leading to extended periods of downtime. This affects your site's availability and can cause a loss of traffic and revenue.

4. **Search Engine Penalties**: Google and other search engines penalize compromised websites by lowering their rankings or removing them from search results altogether. This can severely affect your site's visibility and organic traffic.

How to Secure Your WordPress Site

Securing your WordPress site involves taking proactive steps to minimize the risk of attacks and data loss. Here are key strategies for securing your WordPress website:

1. **Keep WordPress, Themes, and Plugins Updated**: WordPress frequently releases updates that fix bugs, improve functionality, and address security vulnerabilities. Ensuring that your WordPress installation, themes, and plugins are always up to date is one of the simplest yet most effective ways to secure your site.

   o Enable automatic updates for minor WordPress releases (you can do this from the **Settings** > **General** section).

   o Regularly check for plugin and theme updates by visiting **Dashboard** > **Updates**.

2. **Use Strong, Unique Passwords**: Password security is crucial. Use strong, unique passwords for your WordPress admin area, database, FTP accounts, and any other access points. A strong password should contain a combination of uppercase and lowercase letters, numbers, and special characters, and should be at least 12 characters long. Avoid using common words or phrases.

Consider using a password manager like **LastPass** or **1Password** to generate and store complex passwords securely.

3. **Implement Two-Factor Authentication (2FA)**: Two-factor authentication adds an extra layer of security by requiring a second form of verification (such as a code sent to your mobile device) in addition to your password. This significantly reduces the risk of unauthorized access, even if someone manages to steal your password.

You can add 2FA to your WordPress site using plugins like **Google Authenticator** or **Wordfence Security**.

4. **Limit Login Attempts**: Brute force attacks occur when a hacker tries multiple combinations of usernames and passwords to gain access to your site. Limiting login attempts can prevent such attacks by temporarily locking out users who enter incorrect credentials repeatedly.

To limit the number of login attempts on your site, you can install a plugin like Limit Login Attempts Reloaded or Wordfence.

5. **Change Your Login URL**: WordPress's default login URL is www.yoursite.com/wp-login.php. Hackers are well aware of this, and it is often targeted in attacks. Changing the login URL to something unique makes it more difficult for hackers to locate the login page and attempt brute-force attacks.

Plugins like **WPS Hide Login** allow you to change your login URL easily.

6. **Use SSL (Secure Sockets Layer) Encryption**: SSL encryption ensures that data transferred between your website and your users is encrypted, protecting sensitive information like login credentials and payment details. SSL certificates also improve trustworthiness and can boost your site's SEO rankings.

To enable SSL, you will need an SSL certificate. Many hosting providers offer free SSL certificates via **Let's Encrypt**, which can be installed directly through your hosting control panel. After installing the certificate, update your WordPress site's **Settings** > **General** to use HTTPS in the site URL.

Best Security Practices: SSL, 2FA, and Strong Passwords

To keep your WordPress website secure, you need to implement a combination of best practices. These include using SSL certificates for secure communication, enabling two-factor authentication (2FA) for login security, and ensuring that all users use strong and unique passwords.

SSL (Secure Sockets Layer)

SSL encryption is vital for securing sensitive data on your website. It ensures that all information transmitted between your website and its visitors is encrypted, making it difficult for hackers to intercept.

- **Why SSL is Important**: SSL protects user data by encrypting information like login credentials and payment details, making it unreadable to hackers. SSL also improves trust and credibility, especially for e-commerce sites, as visitors can see the padlock symbol next to the URL, indicating a secure connection.

- **Setting Up SSL on Your WordPress Site**: You can easily add SSL to your WordPress site by obtaining an SSL certificate from your hosting provider or using a service like **Let's Encrypt**. Once the certificate is installed, update your site's URLs to use HTTPS by going to **Settings** > **General** and changing both the **WordPress Address (URL)** and **Site Address (URL)** to HTTPS.

Two-Factor Authentication (2FA)

2FA adds an extra layer of protection by requiring a second form of identification in addition to a password. Even if someone steals your password, they won't be able to access your site without the second factor (such as a code sent to your mobile device).

- **Why 2FA is Important**: 2FA significantly reduces the risk of unauthorized access to your WordPress site by requiring an additional verification step, making it harder for hackers to gain entry, even with stolen credentials.

- **Setting Up 2FA**: To implement 2FA, you can install a plugin like **Google Authenticator** or

Authy. These plugins integrate with your WordPress login and require you to enter a time-based code sent to your mobile device before you can log in.

Strong Passwords

Using strong, unique passwords is one of the simplest yet most effective ways to secure your site. Long, complex, and unpredictable passwords are harder for attackers to guess or crack.

- **Why Strong Passwords Matter**: Weak passwords are a common entry point for hackers who rely on brute force methods to guess passwords. Strong passwords make it significantly harder for attackers to gain access to your site.

- **Creating Strong Passwords**: Use a combination of uppercase and lowercase letters, numbers, and symbols. Avoid using easily guessable information like your name or birthdate. Consider using a password manager to generate and store complex passwords.

Installing and Configuring Security Plugins (e.g., Sucuri)

One of the easiest ways to secure your WordPress website is by installing a security plugin. These plugins provide a variety of features, including malware scanning, firewall protection, and login protection, that help protect your site from online threats. One of the most popular and reliable security plugins for WordPress is **Sucuri**.

Sucuri Security Plugin

Sucuri is a comprehensive security plugin that offers a wide range of protection features, including real-time monitoring, malware scanning, and security alerts. Here's how to install and configure Sucuri on your WordPress site:

1. **Install Sucuri**:

   o Go to **Plugins** > **Add New** in your WordPress dashboard.

   o Search for **Sucuri Security** and click **Install Now**.

   o After installation, click **Activate** to enable the plugin.

145

2. **Configure Sucuri**:

    o Once activated, go to **Sucuri Security** in the WordPress dashboard menu.

    o Follow the setup wizard to configure basic security features, including malware scanning, firewall protection, and monitoring.

    o Enable **Security Activity Monitoring** to track user activity and logins.

    o Set up **File Integrity Monitoring** to detect changes to core WordPress files and alert you if anything is modified.

3. **Use Sucuri's Firewall**: Sucuri also offers a cloud-based website firewall that helps protect your site from DDoS attacks, SQL injections, and other types of malicious traffic. You can enable this feature by signing up for Sucuri's premium service.

How to Back Up Your WordPress Site Regularly

Regular backups are essential for ensuring the safety of your website's data. If something goes wrong, such as a security breach, server failure, or accidental deletion of content, having a backup allows you to restore your site to its previous state.

Why Backups are Important

- **Data Recovery**: Having a backup means you can restore your site's data and minimize downtime in the event of a cyber attack or technical failure.

- **Protection Against Human Error**: Sometimes mistakes happen, and content or files can be deleted accidentally. A backup ensures that you can restore the deleted items without data loss.

- **Peace of Mind**: Knowing that your site is backed up regularly provides peace of mind and ensures that you're prepared for any unexpected events.

How to Back Up Your WordPress Site

1. **Install a Backup Plugin**: There are several excellent backup plugins for WordPress, including **UpdraftPlus**, **BackupBuddy**, and **Jetpack**. For instance, to use **UpdraftPlus**:

- Go to **Plugins** > **Add New** and search for **UpdraftPlus**.

- Click **Install Now**, then **Activate**.

- After activation, go to **Settings** > **UpdraftPlus Backups** and choose where to store your backups (e.g., Google Drive, Dropbox, Amazon S3).

- Set up a backup schedule (e.g., weekly or daily) and choose the components of your site to back up (files, database, themes, plugins).

- Click **Backup Now** to create your first backup.

2. **Manual Backups**: You can also back up your site manually by exporting the WordPress database via phpMyAdmin and downloading your website files via FTP. However, using a backup plugin is much easier and more efficient.

Maintaining Your Site: Updates, Cleaning Up Databases, and Monitoring Performance

Once your site is live, ongoing maintenance is necessary to keep it running smoothly, securely, and efficiently. Regular updates, cleaning up databases, and monitoring performance are essential maintenance tasks that ensure the longevity of your site.

Updates

WordPress, themes, and plugins frequently receive updates to fix bugs, improve functionality, and address security vulnerabilities. Failing to keep your site updated can leave it vulnerable to attacks. To manage updates:

- Go to **Dashboard** > **Updates** to check for available updates for WordPress core, themes, and plugins.

- Enable automatic updates for minor WordPress releases.

- Review major updates carefully and test them on a staging site before applying them to your live site.

Cleaning Up Your Database

Over time, your WordPress database can become cluttered with unnecessary data, such as spam comments, post revisions, and expired transients. Cleaning up your database helps improve site performance and reduces the risk of database corruption.

Use plugins like **WP-Optimize** or **WP-Sweep** to clean your database by removing unnecessary

data. These plugins can help you optimize your database tables, delete spam comments, and remove unused options and revisions.

Monitoring Performance

Regularly monitoring your site's performance helps ensure that it's running smoothly and efficiently. Use tools like **Google PageSpeed Insights**, **GTmetrix**, or **Pingdom** to track loading times and identify performance bottlenecks.

- Optimize images to reduce page load times.

- Minimize the use of external scripts and plugins.

- Enable caching and implement a content delivery network (CDN) to speed up your site.

Understanding Website Analytics and How to Track Your Site's Success

Analytics provide valuable insights into your website's performance, including traffic, user behavior, and conversions. By monitoring these metrics, you can make data-driven decisions to improve your site.

Setting Up Google Analytics

Google Analytics is a powerful tool for tracking your website's performance. To integrate Google Analytics with your WordPress site:

1. Sign up for a **Google Analytics** account at analytics.google.com.

2. Add the tracking code to your WordPress site using a plugin like MonsterInsights or manually to your theme's header.php file.

3. Once integrated, Google Analytics will start tracking user visits, page views, bounce rates, and more.

Key Metrics to Monitor

- **Traffic Sources**: Understand where your visitors are coming from (e.g., organic search, social media, referrals).

- **User Behavior**: Track how users interact with your site, including pages viewed, time spent on site, and bounce rates.

- **Conversion Rates**: Measure how many visitors complete desired actions (e.g., making a purchase, signing up for a newsletter).

- **SEO Performance**: Monitor keyword rankings and organic search traffic using Google Analytics and Google Search Console.

By regularly reviewing analytics, you can identify areas for improvement, measure the success of marketing campaigns, and optimize your site's performance.

Maintaining the security, backup, and performance of your WordPress website is an ongoing task that requires careful attention and regular action. By implementing best practices for security, scheduling regular backups, keeping your site updated, and using analytics to track success, you can ensure that your WordPress site remains safe, functional, and optimized for growth. Taking proactive steps to secure and maintain your website will help you avoid potential disruptions and keep your website running smoothly for years to come.

Chapter 11: Troubleshooting Common WordPress Issues

As a WordPress website owner, you'll inevitably encounter issues from time to time. Whether you're dealing with a "White Screen of Death," plugin conflicts, slow performance, or broken links, it's essential to understand how to troubleshoot and resolve common problems. A solid understanding of troubleshooting techniques will help you get your website back up and running quickly, preventing long downtimes and ensuring a smooth user experience for your visitors.

In this chapter, we will explore some of the most common WordPress issues, including errors like the **White Screen of Death** and **404 Errors**. We will also discuss how to troubleshoot plugin and theme conflicts, strategies for handling slow websites, fixing broken links, and effectively dealing with website downtime and errors.

Common Errors and How to Resolve Them

WordPress users commonly encounter several types of errors that can interfere with the normal operation of their website. Some errors are simple to fix, while others require more in-depth troubleshooting. Below are a few of the most common WordPress errors and how to resolve them.

1. White Screen of Death (WSOD)

The **White Screen of Death (WSOD)** is a well-known issue in WordPress that causes the website to display a completely blank white page instead of loading the usual content. Several issues, including plugin or theme conflicts, memory exhaustion, or corrupt files, can cause this problem.

How to Fix the White Screen of Death:

- **Increase PHP Memory Limit**: Often, the WSOD occurs when WordPress exceeds the PHP memory limit. To fix this, you can increase the memory limit by editing the wp-config.php file:

    1. Access your website's root folder via FTP.

    2. Open the wp-config.php file.

3. Add the following line of code just before the line that says, "That's all, stop editing! Happy blogging."

```php
define('WP_MEMORY_LIMIT', '256M');
```

This increases the memory limit to 256MB, which is typically enough to prevent WSOD.

- **Deactivate Plugins**: A faulty or incompatible plugin is often the culprit behind WSOD. Deactivate all your plugins to see if the problem goes away. You can deactivate plugins from the **Plugins** page in the WordPress dashboard, or if you can't access the dashboard, use FTP to navigate to the wp-content folder and rename the plugins folder to something like plugins_backup. Once you've deactivated the plugins, try reactivating them one by one to identify the faulty plugin.

- **Switch to a Default Theme**: If the problem persists, it might be related to your theme. To rule this out, switch to one of the default WordPress themes (like Twenty Twenty-One).

You can do this through the WordPress admin panel under **Appearance** > **Themes**, or by renaming the active theme folder via FTP.

- **Check for PHP Errors**: Sometimes, PHP errors can cause the WSOD. To view the errors, you can enable debugging in WordPress. To do this, add the following lines to your wp-config.php file:

```php
define('WP_DEBUG', true);
define('WP_DEBUG_LOG', true);
```

- These lines will log errors in the wp-content/debug.log file, helping you pinpoint the issue.

2. 404 Errors

A **404 Error** occurs when a page is not found. It can happen when a user tries to access a broken or non-existent URL. This can be frustrating for both users and website owners because it can affect user experience and SEO rankings.

How to Fix 404 Errors:

- **Reset Permalinks**: Sometimes, 404 errors occur due to permalink issues. To fix this, go to **Settings** > **Permalinks** in your WordPress dashboard and click **Save Changes**. This action will flush and regenerate the rewrite rules, fixing most 404 errors.

- **Check for URL Typos**: Double-check the URL of the page generating the error. It's possible that the URL is typographical or that the page has been moved or deleted. If a page has been deleted, consider setting up a redirect to another relevant page.

- **Use Redirection Plugin**: If you've changed the URL structure or deleted pages, you can use the **Redirection** plugin to create 301 redirects, which will point old URLs to new pages. This ensures that visitors don't encounter 404 errors and helps maintain SEO rankings.

3. Internal Server Error (500 Error)

Another common error that makes your site inaccessible is the 500 Internal Server Error. Corrupted .htaccess files, plugin conflicts, or exhausted server resources can trigger it.

How to Fix Internal Server Error:

- **Deactivate Plugins**: As with the White Screen of Death, a plugin conflict can often cause a 500 error. Turn off all your plugins to see if the problem is resolved. If it is, reactivate each plugin one by one to identify the problematic one.

- **Check .htaccess File**: A corrupted .htaccess file can lead to a 500 error. To fix this, rename your .htaccess file (located in the root directory) to something like .htaccess_backup and then try loading your website. If this resolves the issue, go to **Settings > Permalinks** and click **Save Changes** to regenerate a new .htaccess file.

- **Increase PHP Limits**: Sometimes, the server may not have enough memory to process requests. Increasing the PHP memory limit (as described in the WSOD section) or increasing the maximum execution time in your php.ini file might help fix the issue.

4. Connection Timed Out Error

A **Connection Timed Out** error happens when your WordPress site takes too long to load, resulting in a timeout. This is typically caused by hosting issues, such as insufficient server resources or poorly optimized plugins and themes.

How to Fix Connection Timed Out Error:

- **Deactivate Plugins and Themes**: Poorly coded plugins and themes can cause your site to hang. Deactivate them and see if the issue persists. If the issue is resolved, reactivate them one by one to find the culprit.

- **Increase PHP Limits**: If your server is running out of memory or time to process requests, increasing the PHP memory limit and execution time can help.

- **Upgrade Hosting**: If your site is receiving heavy traffic, it may be time to upgrade to a better hosting plan. Shared hosting plans can be restrictive in terms of server resources, so consider upgrading to **VPS** or **Managed WordPress Hosting** for better performance.

How to Troubleshoot Plugin and Theme Conflicts

WordPress plugins and themes often conflict with each other, especially when they are not updated regularly or when they are incompatible with the latest version of WordPress. These conflicts can cause issues like broken pages, layout problems, and even site crashes.

How to Troubleshoot Plugin Conflicts

1. **Deactivate All Plugins**: The first step in troubleshooting plugin conflicts is to deactivate all plugins and check if the issue persists. If deactivating the plugins fixes the problem, reactivate each plugin one by one to identify the conflicting plugin.

2. **Check for Plugin Updates**: Ensure that all plugins are updated to their latest versions. Developers frequently release updates to fix bugs and improve compatibility with the latest version of WordPress.

3. **Use Plugin Conflict Detection Tools**: Some tools can help you detect plugin conflicts. The **Health Check & Troubleshooting** plugin allows you to run your site in troubleshooting

mode, where only essential plugins are enabled, making it easier to identify conflicts.

How to Troubleshoot Theme Conflicts

Theme conflicts can be trickier to diagnose, but there are steps you can take to resolve them:

1. **Switch to a Default Theme**: If you suspect a theme conflict, switch to one of the default WordPress themes (e.g., Twenty Twenty-One) to see if the issue is resolved. If switching to a default theme fixes the problem, the issue likely lies with your active theme.

2. **Update Your Theme**: Check if your theme is up to date. If you're using a custom or third-party theme, you may need to contact the developer for updates or troubleshooting help.

3. **Child Theme Modifications**: If you are using a child theme and have made modifications, try disabling custom code to see if it's causing the issue.

Dealing with Slow WordPress Websites

Slow loading speeds can harm your website's user experience, SEO, and conversion rates. If your WordPress site is slow, it's crucial to diagnose the underlying issues and address them.

How to Improve WordPress Site Speed

1. **Use Caching**: Caching helps reduce server load by storing static versions of your pages. You can use caching plugins like **W3 Total Cache** or **WP Super Cache** to improve your site's speed.

2. **Optimize Images**: Large images can significantly slow down your site. Image optimization tools like Smush or EWWW Image Optimizer can compress images without compromising quality.

3. **Minimize HTTP Requests**: Reduce the number of elements that need to be loaded on each page. This can include minimizing the number of images, scripts, and external resources.

4. **Use a Content Delivery Network (CDN)**: A CDN stores copies of your website's static files on servers around the world, reducing the distance between your site's files and your users, which helps speed up loading times. Popular CDN services include **Cloudflare** and **KeyCDN**.

5. **Upgrade Your Hosting**: If you are using shared hosting, it may be time to upgrade to **VPS hosting** or **Managed WordPress Hosting**, which offer more resources and better performance.

Fixing Broken Links and Ensuring Smooth Website Navigation

Broken links can negatively affect user experience, SEO, and the credibility of your website. They can lead to 404 errors and make it harder for users to navigate your site.

How to Fix Broken Links

1. **Use Broken Link Checker**: Install the **Broken Link Checker** plugin to scan your

website for broken links. This plugin will identify any broken internal and external links on your site, and you can easily fix or remove them.

2. **Redirect Broken Links**: If a page has been removed or relocated, use a plugin like **Redirection** to set up a 301 redirect to a relevant page. This ensures that visitors who try to access the old URL are directed to the right place.

3. **Manually Check Links**: Periodically check your website for broken links, especially after major site changes like theme updates or content restructuring. This is particularly important for blogs and e-commerce sites with constantly changing content.

How to Handle Website Downtime and Errors Effectively

Website downtime is inevitable at times, but how you handle it can make a big difference. Whether it's due to a server issue, maintenance, or a security breach, it's important to act quickly to minimize the impact on your users and customers.

How to Handle Downtime

1. **Use a Uptime Monitoring Service**: Sign up for an uptime monitoring service like **Pingdom** or **Uptime Robot** to receive alerts when your website goes down. This allows you to take immediate action and address the issue promptly.

2. **Implement a Maintenance Mode Page**: If you need to take your site down for updates or maintenance, use a **Maintenance Mode** plugin to display a friendly message to visitors. This ensures users know the site is being worked on and will be back shortly.

3. **Inform Your Users**: If your site experiences extended downtime, inform your users via social media or email. Transparency is key to maintaining user trust.

By understanding how to troubleshoot common WordPress issues, secure your site, optimize performance, and handle downtime effectively, you will be better prepared to maintain a smooth-running website. Troubleshooting is an essential skill for every WordPress website owner, as it ensures that your site stays secure, functional, and user-friendly. This ultimately enhances the overall experience for visitors and improves your site's success.

Chapter 12: Going Live and Post-Launch Best Practices

After months of hard work and careful planning, the day of launching your WordPress website has finally arrived. Going live is a monumental moment, but it's not the end of the process. In fact, the launch of your site marks the beginning of an ongoing effort to maintain, promote, and optimize it for better performance and user experience. This chapter will guide you through essential post-launch practices, including a final checklist before launching, testing your site on different devices and browsers, promoting your website, understanding website analytics tools, and maintaining and updating your site after launch. By following these best practices, you will set yourself up for long-term success and ensure your site thrives post-launch.

Final Checklist Before Launching Your WordPress Site

Before you hit the "publish" button and go live, it's critical to review your website thoroughly to ensure everything is in place. This final checklist will help you make sure you haven't missed any important steps and that your website is ready for the world.

1. Check Your Content

- **Proofread Your Content**: Go through all your pages and blog posts to ensure there are no spelling or grammar mistakes. This step is essential for maintaining professionalism.

- **Ensure All Links Are Working**: Check that all internal and external links are working correctly. Broken links can lead to 404 errors and frustrate visitors, which negatively impacts user experience and SEO.

- **Ensure Content Is SEO-Optimized**: Review your content for SEO. Ensure that each page or post is properly optimized with relevant keywords, meta descriptions, and alt text for images.

- **Images and Media**: Ensure that all images, videos, and other media elements are properly optimized for web use. Images should be compressed to reduce file size without losing quality, as large images can slow down your website.

2. Test Your Website's Functionality

- **Forms and Call-to-Actions (CTAs)**: Test all forms on your site, such as contact forms, sign-up forms, and checkout forms, to ensure they are working correctly. Check that the submissions go to the correct email address and that the forms are submitting successfully.

- **Payment Gateway**: If you have an online store, test your payment gateway to ensure that customers can make purchases smoothly. Ensure that payment processing works properly with various payment methods (e.g., credit cards, PayPal).

- **Test the Search Function**: If your site has a search feature, test it to ensure it is returning relevant results for users.

3. Test Site Performance and Speed

- **Page Speed**: Use tools like **Google PageSpeed Insights** or **GTmetrix** to analyze your website's loading speed. Ensure that your site is loading quickly, as slow websites negatively affect user experience and SEO rankings.

- **Caching**: If you are using caching plugins (such as **W3 Total Cache** or **WP Super Cache**), verify that they are functioning correctly and that your pages load faster for repeat visitors.

- **Minimize HTTP Requests**: Ensure that your website has minimal HTTP requests by reducing the number of elements (scripts, images, etc.) loaded on each page. Tools like **Pingdom** can help identify unnecessary elements causing slow load times.

4. Mobile Responsiveness

- **Mobile Optimization**: With mobile traffic now outpacing desktop traffic, your site must be mobile-friendly. Ensure your website is responsive and adjusts well to different screen sizes. Test all pages on mobile devices to ensure proper layout and functionality.

5. Security Measures

- **SSL Certificate**: Ensure that your site is using SSL encryption. SSL (Secure Sockets Layer) ensures that data is transferred securely between your site and your visitors. Make sure your site's URL begins with **https://** and displays the padlock symbol in the browser address bar.

- **Security Plugins**: Install a reliable security plugin (such as **Wordfence** or **Sucuri**) to protect your site from hacking attempts, malware, and other security threats.

- **Backup System**: Ensure that you have a solid backup system in place. Regular backups are essential in case something goes wrong. Plugins like **UpdraftPlus** or **BackupBuddy** can help you back up your website's data automatically.

Testing Your Site on Different Devices and Browsers

It's essential to test your WordPress website on various devices and browsers to ensure that it works flawlessly for all users. A website that performs well on one device but not on others can lead to a poor user experience, causing visitors to leave your site in frustration.

1. Testing on Multiple Devices

Your website should be responsive, meaning it should adapt to different screen sizes (desktops, laptops, tablets, and smartphones). Test the site on popular mobile devices such as iPhones, Android phones, and various tablet models.

- **Test for Usability**: Check if the text is readable, images are properly displayed, and buttons or forms are easy to interact with on smaller screens.

- **Test for Touchscreen Compatibility**: Ensure that your website's navigation and interactive elements, such as buttons, are responsive to touchscreen interactions.

2. Testing on Different Browsers

Not all users use the same browser, so it's important to test your website's compatibility across various browsers. Focus on the most widely used browsers such as Google Chrome, Mozilla Firefox, Safari, Microsoft Edge, and Opera.

- **Cross-Browser Compatibility Testing**: Use online tools like **BrowserStack** or **CrossBrowserTesting** to test your site across different browsers and devices. These tools allow you to simulate how your site looks and performs on various browsers.

- **CSS and JavaScript Compatibility**: Sometimes, specific CSS properties or JavaScript functions may not work the same across browsers. Test how each element of your website behaves on different browsers, particularly elements such as menus, animations, and pop-ups.

Promoting Your Website: Social Media, Content Marketing, and Email Campaigns

Once your website is live and fully functional, the next crucial step is promoting it. Without promotion, even the most beautifully designed website may remain invisible. Effective promotion strategies, including social media marketing, content marketing, and email campaigns, will help you attract visitors and convert them into loyal customers or subscribers.

1. Social Media Marketing

Social media is one of the most effective tools for driving traffic to your website. By leveraging platforms such as Facebook, Twitter, Instagram, and LinkedIn, you can reach a vast audience and direct them to your site.

- **Create Shareable Content**: Post engaging, shareable content that encourages your followers to share your posts with their networks. Infographics, blog posts, and images are often highly shareable.

- **Use Hashtags**: Relevant hashtags can increase the visibility of your posts on platforms like Instagram and Twitter. Use tools like **Hashtagify** or **RiteTag** to identify trending and relevant hashtags in your niche.

- **Post Regularly**: Consistent posting helps keep your audience engaged and aware of your brand. Use tools like **Buffer** or **Hootsuite** to schedule posts across multiple platforms in advance.

- **Engage with Your Audience**: Respond to comments, direct messages, and questions on your social media channels. Engaging with your followers fosters relationships and encourages them to visit your site.

2. Content Marketing

Content marketing is a powerful strategy for attracting organic traffic and building your brand's authority. By creating valuable and informative content, you can draw visitors to your website and keep them coming back for more.

- **Start a Blog**: Regularly post high-quality blog articles that offer value to your target audience. Share tips, how-to guides, case studies, industry insights, and other content relevant to your business.

- **Optimize Content for SEO**: Optimize your content for search engines by using relevant keywords, adding meta descriptions, and optimizing images. This will help increase your organic search rankings and drive more traffic.

- **Content Promotion**: Share your blog posts on social media and other platforms like LinkedIn or Medium to expand your reach. You can also collaborate with influencers or other businesses in your niche to promote your content.

3. Email Campaigns

Email marketing is one of the most effective ways to maintain relationships with your audience and encourage repeat visits to your site.

- **Build an Email List**: Use tools like **Mailchimp** or **ConvertKit** to build and manage your email list. Offer incentives such as exclusive content, discounts, or a free resource in exchange for email sign-ups.

- **Create Engaging Newsletters**: Send regular newsletters with valuable content, product updates, promotions, or event information. Ensure that your emails are personalized and relevant to your subscribers.

- **Segment Your Email List**: Segment your email list based on user behavior, preferences, or demographics. This allows you to send targeted emails that resonate with each group, increasing the likelihood of engagement.

Understanding Website Analytics Tools (e.g., Google Analytics)

Once your website is live and you begin promoting it, it's crucial to track its performance. Website analytics provide valuable insights into how visitors are interacting with your site, which pages are most popular, where traffic is coming from, and how visitors are converting.

1. Setting Up Google Analytics

Google Analytics is one of the most powerful tools for tracking website performance. It provides comprehensive data on visitor behavior, traffic sources, conversion rates, and more.

- **Install Google Analytics**: To integrate Google Analytics with your WordPress site, sign up for a free account at **Google Analytics**. After you've created your account, you'll receive a tracking code, which you can add to your site. Alternatively, you can use plugins like **MonsterInsights** to make the integration process easier.

- **Set Up Goals**: In Google Analytics, goals allow you to track important actions such as form submissions, product purchases, or email sign-ups. Setting up goals enables you to measure your site's performance in terms of conversions.

- **Monitor Key Metrics**: Track important metrics such as:

  - **Traffic Sources**: Where are your visitors coming from? (e.g., organic search, social media, paid ads)

  - **Bounce Rate**: How many visitors leave your site after viewing just one page?

  - **Pages per Session**: How many pages does a visitor view on average?

  - **Conversion Rate**: How well does your site convert visitors into customers or leads?

2. Google Search Console

Google Search Console is another valuable tool that helps you monitor and optimize your website's presence in Google search results.

- **Submit Sitemaps**: To help Google crawl and index your site more efficiently, submit your website's sitemap to Google Search Console.

- **Check for Crawl Errors**: Review crawl errors and fix any broken links or issues that prevent Google from indexing your pages correctly.

- **Analyze Search Performance**: Google Search Console provides insights into how your site ranks for specific keywords, which pages receive the most impressions, and which queries bring visitors to your site.

Maintaining and Updating Your Site After Launch

Once your site is live, ongoing maintenance is essential to ensure that it continues to run smoothly and securely. Website maintenance involves updating plugins and themes, monitoring performance, performing backups, and ensuring content is current.

1. Regular Updates

- **Update WordPress**: Always keep WordPress updated to the latest version. WordPress regularly releases security patches, bug fixes, and performance improvements.

- **Update Plugins and Themes**: Ensure that all plugins and themes are kept up to date. Outdated plugins and themes can introduce security vulnerabilities and compatibility issues.

2. Security and Backup

- **Backups**: To protect your website's data, set up regular backups. Use plugins like **UpdraftPlus** to schedule daily or weekly backups of your website's content and database.

- **Monitor Security**: Use security plugins like **Wordfence** or **Sucuri** to monitor your website for malware, hacking attempts, and other security threats. Also, scan it regularly for potential vulnerabilities.

3. Performance Monitoring

- **Track Website Speed**: Use tools like **GTmetrix** or **Google PageSpeed Insights** to monitor your website's speed. If your site is slow, consider optimizing images, reducing the number of plugins, and using caching tools to improve load times.

- **Check Mobile Responsiveness**: Regularly test your site's performance on mobile devices. With mobile traffic increasing, mobile-friendly sites are essential for user engagement and SEO.

Going live with your WordPress site is an exciting milestone, but it's just the beginning. By following these post-launch best practices, you can ensure that your site remains functional, secure, and optimized for both users and search engines. Regular testing, promotion, and maintenance are critical for continued success and growth. With the right approach, your website will thrive, attracting visitors, engaging customers, and achieving your online goals.

Conclusion

Throughout this book, we have navigated the full spectrum of WordPress design and development, from setting up your site and customizing its appearance to ensuring its security, performance, and long-term success. WordPress is a powerful, flexible platform, but like any tool, it requires a combination of technical knowledge and practical skills to leverage its potential fully. Whether you are just starting your WordPress journey or have been working with it for some time, this book has provided you with the fundamental skills, techniques, and best practices you need to succeed in building and managing a website on this platform.

In this conclusion, we will recap the key concepts you've learned throughout the book, offer encouragement for continued learning, provide final tips for achieving success with WordPress, and share resources to help you keep growing as a WordPress designer and developer.

Recap of the Key Concepts Learned Throughout the Book

Throughout the book, we explored many essential aspects of WordPress website design and development.

Let's revisit the key concepts that we covered to reinforce your understanding of WordPress:

1. Getting Started with WordPress

In the initial chapters, we introduced you to WordPress, its key features, and the steps to setting up your first site. We discussed choosing a domain name, selecting a hosting provider, and installing WordPress. From there, we explored the WordPress dashboard and its various functions, helping you navigate the interface and become familiar with the settings and options available.

2. Customizing Your Website

Customization is at the heart of WordPress, and we delved into how to make your website uniquely yours. From selecting and installing themes to customizing them using HTML, CSS, and PHP, you've learned how to tweak your site's design and functionality to match your vision. We covered how to use child themes for safe customizations, how to build custom page templates, and how to extend WordPress through custom post types and fields.

3. Optimizing Your Website for SEO

We discussed how search engine optimization (SEO) is crucial for increasing your website's visibility and attracting organic traffic. By utilizing plugins like Yoast SEO, focusing on keyword strategies, and applying best practices like optimizing title tags and meta descriptions, you can ensure your site is optimized for search engines. Speed optimization, mobile responsiveness, and structured data were also covered as part of the SEO landscape.

4. Ensuring Website Security and Backup

Security is an ongoing concern for every WordPress site. We talked about using SSL certificates, setting up two-factor authentication (2FA), using security plugins like Wordfence and Sucuri, and backing up your website regularly to avoid data loss. By implementing these measures, you will protect your site from common threats and ensure it is safe for your visitors and customers.

5. Troubleshooting Common WordPress Issues

WordPress websites are not immune to issues like the White Screen of Death, 404 errors, or slow performance. Throughout the book, we provided troubleshooting techniques for identifying and resolving these common errors, as well as dealing with plugin and theme conflicts. By knowing how to diagnose and fix issues as they arise, you can keep your site running smoothly and avoid prolonged downtime.

6. Launching Your Website and Post-Launch Best Practices

The final stage of any website project is the launch, and we covered the final checklist, testing for mobile responsiveness, and promoting your site through social media, email marketing, and content marketing. Post-launch, we emphasized the importance of maintaining your site by regularly updating themes and plugins, monitoring performance, and reviewing analytics to ensure the ongoing success of your site.

Encouragement for Both Beginners and Professionals to Continue Learning

WordPress is a constantly evolving platform, and there is always more to learn. As a beginner, you may feel overwhelmed at first, but remember that WordPress is designed to be user-friendly, and with practice, you will become more comfortable with its features. For professionals, the world of WordPress development is vast, and there are always new tools, techniques, and best practices to explore. The beauty of WordPress is its flexibility—whether you're designing a simple blog or developing a complex, custom-built site for a client, the possibilities are endless.

For Beginners:

If you are new to WordPress, it may seem like there's a steep learning curve. However, don't be discouraged. Take things one step at a time and gradually build your knowledge. Focus on understanding the basics first: how to install themes, add plugins, and create posts and pages. As you gain confidence, you can start exploring more advanced topics, like customizing your theme, optimizing for SEO, and implementing security measures.

Remember that WordPress is a platform with a huge community of users who have shared their knowledge. Don't hesitate to ask questions, experiment, and explore tutorials online. With persistence, you'll be able to build a strong foundation for your WordPress skills.

For Professionals:

As a professional WordPress designer or developer, your journey doesn't end with a finished project. Stay up-to-date with the latest developments in the WordPress ecosystem, including new themes, plugins, and best practices. Embrace continuous learning and consider exploring areas such as custom plugin development, advanced theme customization, performance optimization, and security auditing.

WordPress also opens the door to a variety of career opportunities, whether you're working with clients, building your portfolio of sites, or offering ongoing website maintenance and optimization services. The key to success as a WordPress professional is a commitment to continuous improvement and staying adaptable as WordPress evolves.

Final Tips for Achieving Success with WordPress Design and Development

Whether you are a beginner just starting your WordPress journey or an experienced developer working on large-scale projects, following best practices and continuing to learn will set you up for success. Here are a few final tips to keep in mind:

1. Start Simple and Build Up

If you are starting, don't try to learn everything at once. Begin with the basics, such as selecting and installing themes, customizing them, and adding content. Once you are comfortable with the platform, move on to more advanced topics like theme development, plugin customization, and performance optimization.

2. Prioritize Mobile Optimization

With mobile traffic accounting for a significant portion of web browsing today, ensure that your WordPress site is mobile-friendly from the start. Choose responsive themes, test your site on various mobile devices, and optimize images and content to load quickly on mobile networks.

3. Focus on Security

WordPress sites are frequent targets for hackers and malicious activity. Implement strong security practices early on—use SSL encryption, choose strong passwords, install security plugins, and perform regular backups. Proactively securing your website will save you time and money in the long run by preventing attacks and data breaches.

4. Test Regularly

Don't wait until something goes wrong to test your website. Regularly test your site on different devices, browsers, and screen sizes to ensure it performs well. Check for broken links, outdated content, and slow-loading pages. Running regular audits of your website's performance and security will help you catch issues before they escalate.

5. Keep Learning

WordPress is a versatile platform with a wealth of learning resources available. Stay updated with the latest trends, tools, and best practices by reading WordPress blogs, following experts on social media, and engaging in forums and communities. The more you learn, the better equipped you will be to handle challenges and create innovative, functional websites.

Resources for Further Learning: WordPress Forums, Blogs, and Communities

WordPress has a thriving community of developers, designers, and users who share their knowledge and experiences through various forums, blogs, and online communities. Here are some valuable resources to continue your learning journey:

1. WordPress.org

The official WordPress website, WordPress.org, is an essential resource for both beginners and professionals. It offers documentation, user guides, plugin and theme repositories, and an active support forum. Whether you need help troubleshooting an issue or want to dive deeper into WordPress development, WordPress.org is a great starting point.

2. WordPress Support Forums

The WordPress Support Forums are a valuable resource for troubleshooting issues and asking questions. You can find solutions to common problems, search for tutorials, or post questions to receive help from experienced WordPress users and developers.

3. WordPress Blogs

- **WPBeginner** (wpbeginner.com): A popular WordPress blog aimed at beginners, offering easy-to-follow tutorials, guides, and tips.

- **WPMU DEV Blog** (wpmudev.com/blog): Offers comprehensive articles on WordPress development, design, and optimization.

- **Torque Magazine** (torquemag.io): Provides news, tutorials, and thought leadership for WordPress professionals.

- **WP Tavern** (wptavern.com): Focuses on news, updates, and trends in the WordPress community, along with in-depth articles on WordPress development and design.

4. Online Communities

- **Reddit WordPress** (r/WordPress): A large community on Reddit where users share news, advice, and resources about WordPress.

- **Stack Overflow** (stackoverflow.com): A popular Q&A website for developers, where you can ask technical questions and find answers from the WordPress development community.

- **Facebook Groups**: There are several WordPress-related groups on Facebook where you can interact with other users, ask for advice, and share tips.

5. Online Learning Platforms

- **Udemy** (udemy.com): Offers a wide range of affordable WordPress courses, covering everything from basic usage to advanced development.

- **LinkedIn Learning** (linkedin.com/learning): Provides high-quality video courses on WordPress design, development, and SEO.

- **WP101** (wp101.com): A platform offering beginner-friendly WordPress tutorials.

Mastering WordPress design and development is a journey that never truly ends. From the initial setup and customization to optimizing performance and security, there is always more to learn, refine, and improve. By following the best practices outlined in this book, you are well on your way to building and maintaining successful, high-quality WordPress websites. Remember that both beginners and experienced users can continuously grow their skills and knowledge, so keep exploring, learning, and experimenting with new ideas. Your WordPress journey is just beginning, and the possibilities are limitless!

Appendices

In this section, we will provide valuable resources to enhance your WordPress journey further, including a list of must-have plugins, additional learning platforms, and a glossary of WordPress terms and jargon. These resources will help you better navigate WordPress, expand your skills, and ensure you stay up-to-date with the latest developments in the WordPress ecosystem.

A. List of Must-Have WordPress Plugins

Plugins are one of the most powerful features of WordPress, allowing you to extend the functionality of your website without having to write custom code. Whether you are building a blog, an e-commerce store, or a business website, the right set of plugins can save you time, increase efficiency, and provide new features that enhance user experience. Below is a list of must-have WordPress plugins that cover essential areas such as security, SEO, performance optimization, backups, and more.

1. SEO Plugins

- **Yoast SEO:**

- Purpose: One of the most popular and comprehensive SEO plugins, Yoast SEO helps you optimize your content for search engines, providing tools for keyword optimization, meta tags, and XML sitemaps.

- Features: Content analysis, meta descriptions, focus keywords, readability check, sitemaps, breadcrumbs, and integration with social media.

- **Rank Math**:

  - Purpose: An alternative to Yoast SEO, Rank Math is a powerful SEO plugin that offers similar features with an intuitive user interface. It is known for being lightweight and easy to use.

  - Features: SEO analysis, rich snippet support, social media integration, and automatic image SEO.

2. Security Plugins

- **Wordfence Security**:

- **Purpose**: Wordfence provides a comprehensive suite of security tools that help protect your site from hacking attempts, malware, and spam.

- **Features**: Firewall, malware scanner, login security, two-factor authentication (2FA), and live traffic monitoring.

- **Sucuri Security**:

  - **Purpose**: Sucuri offers security solutions for WordPress websites, including malware detection, firewall protection, and security monitoring.

  - **Features**: Malware scanning, real-time website monitoring, firewall, and DDoS protection.

3. Backup Plugins

- **UpdraftPlus**:

  - **Purpose**: UpdraftPlus is one of the most popular backup plugins for WordPress, offering both manual and scheduled backups. It supports multiple cloud storage options for safe data storage.

- **Features**: Scheduled backups, cloud storage integration (e.g., Google Drive, Dropbox, Amazon S3), and backup restoration.

- **BackupBuddy**:

  - **Purpose**: BackupBuddy is a premium backup plugin that offers automated backups, one-click restores, and migration features.

  - **Features**: Full site backups, database backups, and cloud integration.

4. Performance Optimization Plugins

- **W3 Total Cache**:

  - **Purpose**: W3 Total Cache is a caching plugin designed to improve site performance by reducing page load times.

  - **Features**: Page caching, database caching, browser caching, and content delivery network (CDN) integration.

- **WP Rocket**:

- **Purpose**: WP Rocket is a premium caching plugin that helps speed up your WordPress website with minimal configuration.

- **Features**: Caching, lazy loading, database optimization, and CDN integration.

- **Smush**:

  - **Purpose**: Smush is an image optimization plugin that helps reduce image file sizes without compromising quality, thereby improving site speed.

  - **Features**: Automatic image compression, lazy loading, and bulk image optimization.

5. Contact Form Plugins

- **Contact Form 7**:

  - **Purpose**: Contact Form 7 is a simple yet flexible plugin that allows you to create and manage multiple forms on your WordPress site.

- o **Features**: Form customization, spam protection (using CAPTCHA), and email integration.

- **WPForms**:

  - o **Purpose**: WPForms is a drag-and-drop form builder plugin that allows you to create various types of forms, such as contact forms, surveys, and payment forms.

  - o **Features**: Drag-and-drop builder, pre-built templates, email notifications, and payment gateway integration.

6. E-Commerce Plugins

- **WooCommerce**:

  - o **Purpose**: WooCommerce is the most popular e-commerce plugin for WordPress, transforming your website into a fully functional online store.

  - o **Features**: Product catalog, shopping cart, secure checkout, payment gateway integration, and inventory management.

- **Easy Digital Downloads (EDD):**

  o **Purpose**: EDD is a plugin specifically designed for selling digital products on WordPress.

  o **Features**: File management, payment gateways, customer management, and discount codes.

7. Analytics Plugins

- **MonsterInsights:**

  o **Purpose**: MonsterInsights integrates Google Analytics with WordPress, providing easy-to-understand reports and insights directly in your WordPress dashboard.

  o **Features**: Real-time traffic tracking, e-commerce tracking, affiliate link tracking, and enhanced e-commerce features.

- **Google Analytics Dashboard for WP:**

  o **Purpose**: This plugin adds a Google Analytics dashboard to your WordPress admin area, making it easy to view traffic data and performance.

- o **Features**: Basic Google Analytics integration, real-time stats, and detailed traffic reports.

8. Social Media Plugins

- **Social Warfare**:

  - o **Purpose**: Social Warfare is a social sharing plugin that helps you add customizable social sharing buttons to your WordPress site.

  - o **Features**: Customizable buttons, click-to-tweet functionality, social analytics, and share counters.

- **Simple Social Icons**:

  - o **Purpose**: Simple Social Icons is a lightweight plugin that allows you to add social media icons to your WordPress website easily.

  - o **Features**: Customizable icon colors, size adjustments, and responsive design.

B. Additional Resources and Learning Platforms

Continuous learning is essential for anyone working with WordPress, whether you're a beginner or an experienced developer. Below are some excellent resources, learning platforms, and communities to help you improve your WordPress skills and stay updated on the latest developments.

1. WordPress Documentation

- **WordPress Codex** (codex.wordpress.org): The WordPress Codex is the official documentation resource for WordPress. It contains detailed guides, tutorials, and best practices for WordPress users at all levels.

- **WordPress Developer Resources** (developer.wordpress.org): This comprehensive resource for developers offers information on theme development, plugin development, API usage, and more.

2. Online Learning Platforms

- **Udemy** (udemy.com): Udemy offers a variety of affordable WordPress courses, ranging from beginner-friendly tutorials to advanced WordPress development and e-commerce training.

- **LinkedIn Learning** (linkedin.com/learning): LinkedIn Learning offers in-depth video courses on WordPress design, development, and optimization, taught by industry professionals.

- **WP101** (wp101.com): WP101 is an excellent resource for beginners, offering high-quality, easy-to-follow video tutorials on WordPress.

3. Forums and Communities

- **WordPress Support Forums** (wordpress.org/support): The official WordPress support forums are a great place to ask questions, find solutions to common problems, and connect with the WordPress community.

- **Reddit – r/WordPress** (reddit.com/r/WordPress): A vibrant WordPress community on Reddit where users share tips, ask questions, and discuss the latest news and trends in the WordPress ecosystem.

- **Stack Overflow** (stackoverflow.com): A widely used platform where developers ask and answer technical questions related to WordPress development.

- **WPBeginner Facebook Group** (facebook.com/groups/wpbeginner): A popular Facebook group for WordPress users to share tips, advice, and tutorials.

4. Blogs and Websites for Learning WordPress

- **WPBeginner** (wpbeginner.com): WPBeginner is an excellent resource for beginners, offering tutorials, product reviews, and guides on all aspects of WordPress.

- **Torque Magazine** (torquemag.io): Torque is a blog dedicated to WordPress news, trends, and tutorials, with contributions from top WordPress developers and professionals.

- **WPMU DEV Blog** (wpmudev.com/blog): The WPMU DEV blog offers expert advice on WordPress design, development, security, and optimization.

- **WPExplorer** (wpexplorer.com): WPExplorer offers tutorials, theme and plugin reviews, and tips for WordPress users.

C. Glossary of WordPress Terms and Jargon

To help you navigate the world of WordPress, we've compiled a glossary of common terms and jargon that are essential to understanding WordPress. Whether you're a beginner or an experienced user, understanding these terms will help you communicate more effectively and better grasp the nuances of WordPress.

1. Admin Dashboard:

The central hub of your WordPress site where you manage your content, settings, plugins, themes, and more. The dashboard is accessed by logging into the WordPress backend.

2. Blogroll:

A list of links to other websites, typically displayed in the sidebar of a WordPress blog. A blogroll is usually used to display a list of favorite blogs or websites.

3. Cache:

A mechanism that stores data temporarily to speed up website loading times. Caching reduces the time it takes to load pages by saving frequently accessed data in memory.

4. Child Theme:

A theme that inherits the functionality of a parent theme but allows for customizations and modifications without affecting the parent theme. Child themes are essential for making safe customizations.

5. Custom Post Types (CPT):

Custom content types that extend the default WordPress post and page types. For example, if you run a website for a restaurant, you could create a custom post type for "menus."

6. Database:

A structured collection of data stored on a server. WordPress uses a MySQL database to store content, user data, comments, and settings.

7. Plugin:

A piece of software that extends the functionality of WordPress. Plugins add new features to your site, such as SEO optimization, contact forms, and e-commerce functionality.

8. Permalink:

The permanent URL structure for a page or post on your WordPress site. A permalink is typically designed to be clean, user-friendly, and SEO-optimized.

9. Shortcodes:

Simple code snippets that allow you to add dynamic content or functionality to posts or pages without needing to write complex code. Shortcodes are enclosed in square brackets, like [gallery].

10. SSL (Secure Sockets Layer):

A protocol for encrypting data between the user's browser and your website. SSL ensures that sensitive information, like login credentials and payment data, is transmitted securely.

11. Theme:

A collection of files that control the design and layout of your WordPress website. Themes define how your site looks and how content is presented to users.

12. Widget:

Small blocks of content or functionality that can be added to the sidebar or other areas of your website. Widgets can display things like recent posts, categories, or social media feeds.

13. WordPress Multisite:

A feature that allows you to run multiple WordPress websites from a single WordPress installation. This is useful for creating a network of sites with shared users and settings.

14. XML Sitemap:

A file that lists all the pages on your website, helping search engines crawl and index your site more efficiently. XML sitemaps are crucial for SEO.

WordPress offers an extensive toolkit for building and managing websites, from installation and customization to optimization and security. By leveraging plugins, learning resources, and the powerful features of WordPress, you can create high-quality websites for any purpose, from personal blogs to complex e-commerce stores. With the glossary, plugin recommendations, and learning resources provided, you are well-equipped to continue growing as a WordPress user, developer, or designer. Happy building!

www.ingramcontent.com/pod-product-compliance
Lightning Source LLC
LaVergne TN
LVHW051229050326
832903LV00028B/2300